LIVING OFF THE GRID

A BEGINNERS GUIDE ON HOW TO GET BACK TO BASICS AND START LIVING A SIMPLE, SUSTAINABLE AND SELF-SUFFICIENT LIFESTYLE.

HOWARD THOMAS

D1607889

FREE BONUS BOOK

GET FREE, UNLIMITED ACCESS TO THIS BOOK PLUS ALL OF OUR NEW BOOKS BY JOINING THE ECO KOALA FAMILY

JUST SCAN THE QR CODE BELOW

CONTENTS

INTRODUCTION

Have you ever felt like you belong in the solitude of nature rather than the bustling hubbub of a city? Have you ever created something from scratch, maybe a fence, or even something as simple as a loaf of bread, and felt the thrill of pride and accomplishment afterward? Have you ever wondered what it would be like to get away from it all and live life the way you want to?

These feelings and desires aren't as uncommon as you might think, but many people don't even realize that there is an alternative to the crazy, merry-go-round life most Americans are locked into. How many people have you heard complain that all they seem to do is work, usually for a job they despise, and then go home and sleep? Moreover, our future seems doomed to be filled with lab-grown meat, GMO crops, invasive government and the elimination of privacy. Is this the kind of world our kids will grow up to inherit? Is this really the only future available to us? Families all over the world are concerned with these things, especially those who live in the United States. As capitalism thrives and individual lives suffer, families are deciding how they want their years to pan out and what kind of legacy they want to pass on.

The good news is that the status quo is changing in this day and age. The "9-5 job" is becoming a thing of the past, especially after the pandemic. More people are deciding to take control of their own lives, including how they work and how they live, and many have begun to discover that there are other options.

The comfort and convenience of being locked into the standard system of our country is alluring. Still, all of these comforts and conveniences seem to be coming at an increased price to health, wellness and freedom. People from all backgrounds and affiliations are taking notice and taking action. They are making the decision to get off the grid.

Living off grid may not share many of the modern day conveniences, and yet, people are flocking in droves to transition into this lifestyle. This drive is coming from a desire to break away from the established systems that many of us disagree with but live within anyway. Living off grid is a new path to freedom in this modern age. It gives back control of things that we have long had control over but only recently have lost!

From the beginning of the human race until about 200 years ago, we controlled how we lived our lives. We knew how our food was made and where it came from because we made it ourselves or personally knew the person who made it. We learned all of the skills we needed to be self-sufficient and independent. We heated our homes and taught our own children. We owned land and animals. We kept in tune with the planet we live on.

Today, as we have drifted away from that lifestyle, we have become a different kind of human race.

Are you ready to get back to the way we used to be?

Are you ready to get back on the human path?

Look, living off grid is not all honey and tulips! We will talk about the advantages and disadvantages of this lifestyle. Frankly, some people are just not cut out for this kind of challenge. However, since you are here reading this book, I think it means that you are! Get ready to dig into all that it takes to get started in off grid living.

You will learn about choosing quality land for your off grid homestead, because not all land is created equal. The right piece of land will have perfect conditions for living off grid and others will struggle to meet your needs. If you don't know what kind of land to buy, then your off grid dream could become something of a nightmare.

We are going to get into a variety of living spaces and homes that you could consider. Living off grid offers up a lot of options; it is not just about living in a wood cabin. As you carry on learning about off grid life, you will find that there are many more options in all of this. Every aspect of off grid living comes with a whole host of choices. You are rarely left to do things one way and one way only.

That is what makes the off grid life so appealing. In many ways, you have more choices living off grid than you do tethered to the power system and municipal services. Nowadays, we are led to believe that our lives are best lived in a city suburb so that we can argue about which restaurant we are going to on Friday night.

Beyond location and home, we will also look at power generation. Even though you are going off grid you will still want to generate power for essentials like lights, charging cables and entertainment sources. Maybe something like an electric coffee maker is one of the items that you miss and would like to power. There is a lot more out there than the sun to power your homestead. We will look at a collection of renewable energies and how to leverage them on your homestead.

After we have covered off grid energy needs, we need to consider what we are going to have walking around on four legs, or two. One of the biggest benefits to buying a home and a piece of land for an off grid homestead is the ownership of food production. Suddenly, you have the power to control your food supply from the field to your plate. That is a special kind of freedom.

A small flock of quail and chickens can provide you with so much food. These little egg factories will pop about an egg a day into the coop. Now imagine having a flock of 20 quail and 20 chickens. You will have so many eggs you won't know what to do with them. You can butcher a chicken or some quail here and there and you will have meat resources, too!

Poultry is hardly the end of the line when it comes to the types of animals that you can keep on your off grid homestead. The great thing about animals is that they have no concerns about electricity. Whether a flock lives outside a mansion with all the lights on or on an off grid homestead burning beeswax candles, they really don't care.

Life off grid is going to take you off of municipal or city water systems. Of course, there are millions of people who live off of major city or municipal water systems. You will likely drill a well as your main water resource, but we will discuss a number of other ways that you can source water from the natural world to assure you have all you need.

The management of your land is another massive part of the off grid lifestyle. How you deal with human and product waste can be quite different for those off grid. Drainage and managing your land responsibly are other important parts of managing that land. We had to learn a lot about managing our land on our own off grid homestead. Let us help you!

Compost is a manner of managing leaves and scraps that will turn these waste items into food for your plants and gardens. You don't need to be off grid to make compost, but I am always interested in the fact that more people don't compost their leaves. Instead, they bag them up and leave them on the curb for cities to pick up. Even when we lived in a city environment, we not only used all of our leaves to compost, but we would take some of the bags of our neighbors' leaves to add to that compost pile! These leaves are like gold that falls from the sky each year!

If we stopped there, this would be one heck of a comprehensive guide. However, one of my favorite parts of getting off grid was learning a collection of new skills to fit your new lifestyle. Many of these skills like using an ax, blacksmithing, woodworking and a never ending list of repair skills were all things that I never thought I could do. Until the challenge was laid before me, I just avoided these kinds of skills. Off grid life will challenge you to become something that you never even knew possible, and I promise you, it's a very fulfilling undertaking.

Some of those skills can even translate into money! Dollars and cents can be the outcome of many chickens or eggs, it can come from blacksmithing, handmade soaps and candles. If you decide to take your off grid journey to the more industrious side, there are lots of opportunities for that. We will also talk about how you can start making money while off grid.

This book is going to be a personal look at what it takes to start living off grid. You are going to be presented with personal stories and information from our experience. I have been gardening, raising animals, and living off the land for nearly a decade and in that time, I have learned so much. It's time to share the stories in a book just like this.

You will hear about some great successes and you will hear about some terrible failures that we have overcome. Getting off grid is anything but easy, so this book will not be all about the good times. Our bad times will help you avoid the pitfalls that are always out there.

At this point, there is nothing left to do but start this book and begin your own journey. You don't have to be sitting on a lot of rural land to read this book or these next few chapters. However, they will take you on an internal journey. They will invite some deep thought into your mind and maybe even a degree of adventure could arise.

Take the first steps. Consider what your life could truly be if you decided to break free from the convenience and benefits of being linked to a city or a suburban area. These perceived benefits are just not all they are cracked up to be. They are also not free. In fact, they are part of a tightening control that seems to desire only complete dominance.

Now is a great time to break free of that control!

WHAT DOES LIVING OFF THE GRID MEAN?

Coffee is one of those reminders that we are still connected. It's not a plant that we can grow on our property, but it's something we drink each day. Though we are off grid, we still need the greater grid and supply chain to get us some of our favorite things.

However, I sit in the morning with a cup of hot coffee and look out onto my land. I see a mist rising off the fields and birds starting to swoop in. Cardinals and jays are bouncing around on spindly legs.

A simple overhead light is burning from the batteries charged by our solar panels. My laptop is on and charged fully from that same power of the life giving sun. In the air is the smell of coffee but also crisping bacon. We didn't buy it at a store. It was given to us by a friend close by who I made a set of coat hooks for on my anvil.

The family is asleep and most of our animals are, too. It's in these moments that I get to write and reflect about what it truly means to live off grid. My kids are going to wake up and eat bacon, toast and eggs that were made right here at home. The eggs came from our coop, the bacon down the street and my wife made the sourdough bread. That's what it means to live off the grid.

If I chose to turn on the depressing news, I would be greeted with a number of stories that would make me hurt for the people who live in tight urban environments, the people who require that all their needs be met by an 18 wheeler and the goods packed on the back of it. In addition, the sparse levels of law and order that once controlled the worst elements in our society seem to be slipping. However, I am here, away from all of that, sipping my coffee on my land.

When the power goes out, my lights stay on. When there is chaos in the streets of our cities, I walk outside and hear the cicadas. If we are headed down the path toward a volatile and uncertain future, I know that I can care for and feed my family. I know they are safe, and I know they have a future because it's in my hands, not a politician's or a supply chain's. This is what it means to be off the grid.

Of course, that is what living off grid means to me. In this chapter, we need to also discuss what it actually means to live off grid. There are many aspects of off grid living that can be confusing.

- How far off grid do you need to be?
- What are the qualifications for being off grid?
- What if I want to be partially off grid?

We are going to touch on these questions and many others that you might have about off grid living and what it means in this chapter. However, to answer all of these questions we have to first look into where the phrase comes from. Getting 'off the grid' has a very literal meaning that may be lost on some of our readers. So, we are going to take a look at what the GRID really is and what we are all trying to get away from.

WHAT IS THE GRID?

To be blunt, the power grid is one of the great marvels of modern engineering that has changed everything for humanity. Our ability to deliver electricity to customers at great distances has increased the quality of life in such an exponential way that it is almost impossible to fathom!

It's a simple system to understand.

1. **Power Plants** of some form or fashion generate the massive amounts of electricity needed to power an area.
2. That power is then run to a **Transmission Substation** which shoots it out in many directions to **High Voltage Transmission Lines.** These are the big power lines that you see in carved out paths across the nation.
3. These power lines lead to **Power Substations.**
4. The power is sent from substations to **Transformers.**
5. Then it is run along power lines to **Transformer Drums** before being run into your home.

When you are tethered to this system you are essentially ON GRID and dependent on the grid. Now, we could also consider the public water system as part of a grid. The sewer system and the clean water systems that pump fresh water into our home and allow us to flush out waste and waste-water are part of the grid, too.

When you are talking about grids you could make a claim that the roads themselves, in a city are their own type of transportation grid. Stores and malls are another form of grid. The collective convenience and essential services of a city or town make up this GRID that many people have become accustomed to.

HOW DID THE WORLD BECOME ELECTRIFIED?

In the 1880s, there was a war going on in the United States, but not the kind you're probably thinking of. It was then that Thomas Edison and Nikola Tesla (yes, the guy the car is named after!) became embroiled in the "War of the Currents." Thomas Edison was the inventor of DC (Direct Current) power, the most popular means of delivering power during that time period. However, it was not the power source that was needed to power the great cities of our nations because of its inflexibility. DC power lacked the ability to create a transmission over a great distance and that meant that very few places had coal-derived electric power in that time.

Tesla's AC (Alternating Current) power, however, seemed to be the solution to the struggles of DC power. The 3 phase system of alternating current was a marvel capable of bringing whole regions and cities power; it was a ground-breaking change! But popular, wealthy Edison was threat-ened by the cheaper, more efficient AC power, and so he effectively discredited Tesla and his work. Therefore, it wasn't until the late 19th and early 20th century that AC power was proved to be a much better means of powering our nation.

Samuel Insull was a popular, influential businessman and innovator during the late 1800s and early 1900s. Think of him as the Henry Ford of electricity. His goal was to focus on things like decreasing the price and increasing accessibility of power to the average American home. It was his thinking and planning that allowed the country to achieve huge steps in becoming completely electrified. That is a very impressive notch in the belt. Now, we exist in a world that could not be without a massive power grid, and this man was the one to truly make that happen.

It is important for you to understand just how much our society needs the power grid. Everything, from how we communicate to how we get clean drinking water, is dependent on the power grid. Our food, water, safety, health, wellness, security and almost everything else are dependent on electricity. Without it, our society would fall into utter chaos in a matter of days or weeks, at most.

Think about it. How well would you cope without electricity right now?

SO, WHY GET OFF THE GRID?

It's easy for such great marvels like the power grid that offer incredible convenience to become something we completely depend on. Of course, the last piece of that puzzle is for unscrupulous people to take advantage of that dependence. Many are 100% dependent on the power grid. This means it can be used against us, too!

A simple terrorist attack on the grid can put hundreds of thousands of people in the dark. An overzealous government can shut off the power on you if you are not doing what they feel you should be doing. This happened in California to people who were disobeying COVID-19 restrictions and having parties. Were they being responsible humans and Americans by meeting in large groups? Well, that's your call. However, the idea that the government can PUNISH you by taking away your electricity doesn't sit well with many.

In January 2021, in the state of Florida, a hacker briefly seized control of a county water system. The hacker adjusted the system to increase the sodium hydroxide in the water system. Sodium hydroxide is lye and is used, in small amounts, to treat water. In high amounts it is extremely dangerous because it is caustic.

The change in the system's setting was caught by the operator and changed back to the appropriate levels before the water supply was affected. This is a real life example of how a small attack on just one aspect of the GRID can affect lots of people. How many people would have died or gotten sick if that hacker were successful?

Conservation of the planet's resources and caring for Earth is a noble goal. However, in the name of climate change we have given ourselves over to desperation, and that is a dangerous place to be. The power grid will be more controlled and your freedom to power, heat and cool your home the way you see fit will slowly be taken from you. This will be done in the name of saving the planet. If you are okay with that then you have nothing to worry about, but if that doesn't sit well with you then it sounds like you would prefer to have control over your own systems.

Despite all of that, we do have some form of responsibility for our planet and the way we have been living has hardly been as good stewards for the world that we are born into. We are part of this planet and we can never forget that. However, we only recently realized our power to affect the planet with our actions. Throughout most of history, it was the planet that had its way with us!

Around 1960 we started to understand that we were having a devastating effect on our planet and that long term we would have to change course if we were going to live a more sustainable existence on this planet. Here we are just 60 years later, and most people understand the importance of getting things in order to help our planet—but it won't be easy. In such a short amount of time, we've become so dependent on all of those things that are hurting the planet that it will be difficult for many to give up these small comforts. Even just the use of so much electricity is heating up the planet, which has been catastrophic for our oceans and even just our weather in general.

Getting off grid might mean powering your home with solar panels as well as powering it more efficiently. We leave lots of things on in our home that just don't need to be left on. When you get off grid, you concern yourself with how much the sun is out and how it might affect the energy your home produces. Maybe you harness wind or waterpower, too, so you can have plenty of access to power.

Being off grid often removes you from the massive amount of packaging that accrues from a life at the supermarket, too. Packaging is another thing that is choking the world around us; chances are, you've seen one of those massive landfills jam-packed with all of our waste, and some of that stuff will take hundreds of years to decompose. When you produce more of your own foods and snacks and become more self-sufficient, you leave less of an imprint on this earth. In fact, you often give back to it!

There is also a great level of freedom that we all can enjoy by getting off grid. It is that voice that calls to us all to be more in tune with the world around us. While the convenience of the electrified and cemented world around us is very alluring, it has taken us away from what it means to be a human. This is one of the strongest reasons to get off grid.

HOW FAR OFF THE GRID?

There are varying degrees of self-sufficiency that you can attain. These are often characterized by how far off grid you go and some other things. We will talk about those other characteristics below. A close friend of mine lives in North Carolina and is about as off grid and self-sufficient as I have ever seen. Her advice changed everything for me. She said, "It's not really possible to be 100% self-sufficient." In my experience, she is 100% right!

The idea that you are going to make, grow and process all the things you need on your land is usually a matter of DAYLIGHT! It is just a lot of work to get everything done. There are also some tremendous skill sets to learn if you are going to be 100% self-sufficient. However, you don't even have to come close to that in order to take advantage of being off grid.

Let's look at the varying degrees of off grid living that should be considered if you want to take this journey.

URBAN PARTIALLY OFF GRID HOMESTEADER

The first class of off grid living might sound like something that is done more out of appearances, but I would warn you not to take a serious urban homestead for granted. The things that people are pulling off on ½ an acre is pretty miraculous!

. . .

Many off grid urban homesteaders are hardly 100% off the grid but they use things like wind power and solar power to affect their monthly power bill. Some of them even sell power back to the power company, but this requires them to be tied into the power grid to do so.

Beyond the aspects of power output, they are also very capable in terms of being able to produce food on their small plot. With things like rabbits, chickens, greenhouses and gardens, a lot can be done on very little space in the right suburban lot.

You won't have the wide open spaces, but you will have much more control over how you power your home and feed your family.

SUBURBAN OFF GRID HOMESTEADER

In the suburbs, things tend to get a little more comfortable. You get more space, and you can really start getting things done as a homesteader. With wide open spaces and less blocking of the sun, you can really crank up the solar power. You might find that you can power most of your home if not all of it! Your heating and cooling systems are often a challenge, but with the right amount of power, you can achieve anything.

A suburban property is also less restrictive from a zoning and other laws perspective. You will be able to use your space to keep more beneficial animals and expand gardens.

Rain barrels and water catchment are much more acceptable in these areas.

If you are more interested in space and limited restrictions, this is the move you want to make. You can be nearly 100% off grid in a suburban setting if you don't get wrapped up in a community with HOA (Homeowner's Association) restrictions.

Take your time finding the right place and you can do really big things and cut the cord of the grid while still being close to convenience areas, if that is your goal.

100% RURAL OFF GRID HOMESTEADER

For many of you this is the ultimate goal. You want to be far away from everything and untethered to anything. There is a boatload of allure here, but you also have to understand that this is a lifestyle change! Most people don't live and have not lived this way. This is a serious kind of isolation.

In a rural setting like this, you can pretty much pull off anything you want! Any kind of energy and any kind of growing or raising of animals is at your fingertips. Where you are basically limited by your land and your space in the previous types of off grid homesteading, here you are limited only by how much you can put into it.

. . .

When you are rural and off grid you will be responsible for everything. Trash, water, waste, power and disaster response, to name a few big ones, is what you will be dealing with. This is another big change if you are from a city or suburb.

MOBILE OFF GRID LIVING

There is one final group of modern off grid pioneers. These are the folks who live on boats, RVs, modified school buses and even vans! This mobile off grid life is built for a certain kind of wandering soul. It allows you to live off the grid while traveling the nation and the world to see the sights.

Another benefit of mobile off grid living is that you can take your time seeking out land, buying it, and eventually building on it. I have seen some incredible school buses that have insulated and outfitted to resemble a modern tiny home on wheels.

When it comes to off grid living it truly is up to the imagination and the drive of the person or people involved.

THE FUTURE OF OFF GRID AND SUSTAINABLE LIVING

With world governments working together to create a zero emissions and sustainable population, there is no doubt that more and more people are going to be moving in the direction of off grid living. Manufacturing will likely be moving in this direction, too. Cars and homes are going to be produced with these goals in mind. To jump off the grid now is to merely stay ahead of that curve and to do it your own way rather than have it forced upon you. With government power, influence and dollars, the world will eventually be forced in this direction. We should be good stewards of our planet and resources on our own; it should not be something that must be dictated to us by a government.

The food supply is headed for big changes, too. These changes will become something you cannot avoid before long. We are moving away from large scale factory farming, particularly with beef. Cow farts are in the reticle of those who are obsessed with emissions, too!

Are you willing to act to get off grid or are you prepared to be acted upon? This is the question that we all must answer when it comes to our future. As the pressure mounts in our nation, many more people will be given to the philosophy of, "Just leave me alone!" That is a good mantra for those who want to live off grid.

. . .

Now, let's get down to business. It's time to start looking at the hard advantages and disadvantages of getting off grid. There are many things to consider, so we will spend the next chapter breaking that down.

2

ADVANTAGES & DISADVANTAGES

When you start your life off grid, even your home starts to look different after a while. Herbs are drying over our sink and hanging from our walls. Rather than cans in the pantry, there are mason jars filled with the harvests of years past. Our curtains are hung on a piece of steel I folded decoratively with a hot forge and an anvil.

. . .

What once felt strange and new becomes part of your daily life. Feeding the goats, gathering the eggs, tending to gardens, it all becomes part of a daily routine. When the time comes and you want a break, well, you gotta find a pretty understanding house sitter! Vacation is something that you might not be able to do as much as you like, or at least not the way you're used to.

An off grid lifestyle will offer you and your family all kinds of benefits. It will change the way you live, eat and look at the world. It will literally change the effect you have on the world! However, it is not all sunshine and lavender. There are some serious disadvantages to off grid living, too. Let's look at both!

DISADVANTAGES OF LIVING OFF GRID

Let's get the hard stuff out of the way first. This is where you have to go mentally to understand the limits of what you are willing to take on. You might find that some of these are deal breakers for you and if that's the case then I can save you a bunch of reading in the chapters to come.

When it comes to off grid living, you are responsible for everything! You might think that is pretty similar to home ownership but there are some serious differences. Of course, in a home in the burbs, you can call a repairman to take care of your problems or you can get a neighbors' help. When you are living off the grid, you might be very rural and all but on your own. That is something to remember!

. . .

If something in your solar power system stops working, you are going to have two options. The first is to get to work and fix the issue on your end; hopefully, you have spare parts. The second is to sit in the dark until you work up the energy to step up and complete option one! So, you don't have a lot of choices when it comes to taking action.

The conveniences that you might enjoy now are going to get further and further out of touch. If you like to eat pork fried rice on a Friday that is delivered by a smiling delivery boy, well that might not be a possibility. There are limits to how far out the deliveries go. Your off grid homestead might be off the delivery grid, as well.

As I mentioned at the beginning of the chapter, taking vacations becomes much more of a challenge. It's not a matter of locking up the home and boarding an airplane to paradise for a week! That is not possible. You have all kinds of living creatures and processes that you are responsible for. You have to find yourself a really special person who is going to take care of your home while you are gone. In fact, your best bet will be a person who is basically willing to live in your home while you are gone.

That adds a level of concern to the whole picture. Now, we are on vacation, but we have animals to concern ourselves with the whole time! We have people in our home, and it gets pretty strange. So, vacation will never be the same. It's not to say it won't be possible, it's just to say that it will not be as easy as it once was.

. . .

One of the most astounding things that happens to you might be both an advantage and a disadvantage. This is a hard one to explain but it's real, so you need to consider it. There are things that you love, right now, that you will not even think of in the future. There are foods, activities, and entertainment that will all but disappear from your life.

What's more is that it will not only go away, but you won't miss it! Maybe you loved football or your favorite fast food chain and you couldn't imagine life without it. Sometimes living off the grid makes your desire for these things go away because you are too busy, you don't have TV or you get used to eating a certain way and you find yourself not even wanting the old treats that you used to. This can be an advantage and a disadvantage.

Feed is another part of your life that will balloon, and you may look at it as a serious issue that you might consider a disadvantage. You see, if you have a bunch of animals on your off grid homestead, well, you are going to need to feed these animals. That could be chicken feed, turkey feed, hay for goats, feed for other types of birds or ungulates but you will need feed all the time.

Of course, there are other new costs to consider, too. Setup cost of new power systems will be good investments but still could be lots of money up front. If these systems break you will have to pay for materials and learn to fix them, as mentioned. The only way to avoid these greater costs is maintenance.

You become the maintenance man for your home, water, power and all other systems. That means that you not only must fix things when they break but you also need to keep up with these systems. Each month you will likely be inspecting one of these systems to assure it has all it needs.

Finally, you will learn to live with much less. You will learn to make or find the things you need rather than head over to Target to buy them. It's interesting because it doesn't happen to be a money issue for most; it happens to be an issue of convenience. It will simply become easier for you to do without something silly that you always thought you "needed" than to drive miles and miles to a store and pay out the nose for it.

ADVANTAGES OF LIVING OFF GRID

With the hard part over we can really enjoy all the overwhelming advantages of living off grid.

What first comes to mind and stands out greater than anything is freedom. It is not hard to recognize that being in control of your power generation and your food and water supply, to some degree, is always going to have massive benefits compared to being dependent on others for those things. When you grow food and power your home with the sun it offers up a real sense of freedom to you and all who are involved.

Next is the experience. Many people find themselves making plenty of money, living in the best homes with all the creature comforts, but they are dragging their feet through the experience like zombies! They are living in a strange, self-imposed hell. That is because their experience is packaged. It's a checklist life and they have already checked all the boxes.

Life on an off grid homestead is an adventure. It's hard work and it's rewarding but it's also an adventure where you are doing new things, experiencing a different kind of life. This is radically beneficial for your children. They get to grow up in a world that is like something out of a movie. They will blow people's minds and they will learn incredible lessons. Most importantly, your children will know what it looks like to be self-reliant.

The cost of prepackaged, maximum comfort living is way up there. Americans are far too unhappy for all the money we spend on living! Off grid living naturally cuts down on living expenses by affecting the power bill and the grocery bill. These things you will see immediately. Not all your endeavors on the off grid homestead will prove profitable, but the quality and the cost work themselves out. Off grid living is a lifestyle change and you will quickly see that things you spent money on in the past become less and less of a priority. Better to spend a sunny day outside in the garden than in the house watching Netflix.

When your home is filling up with food from just outside your window, it's easy to get all romantic and excited about the prospect of off grid living. Not only will your fields become full of food but so will your pantries. There will be no more questions about where your food comes from. It will come from right outside your window.

Our style of living in this nation is becoming toxic for our planet. We do not manage packaging well; we are tremendously wasteful, and the world suffers for our sins. We don't feel it when the trash leaves our home, but another environment somewhere else does. We don't feel it when the pollution from the coal plant is pushed high into the sky to generate our electricity, but our atmosphere does.

Living off grid will naturally push you in the direction of being more conscious about your effects on the planet. While it might seem like people have become a virus on the planet, it was not until around 1960 that we realized we had become a force that could affect the entire planet. So, we have done a lot to steer the ship in the right direction since then.

The biggest effect will always come from the actions of the individual each and every day. When you begin living a lifestyle of self-reliance and independence, you start to lessen your effects on the planet. This comes from day to day eating, drinking, powering and the literal effect you have on the soil around you! The actual planet beneath your feet gets made better when you prep fields for pasture or when you prep soil for gardening.

We have been creatures that have existed on our own blood, sweat and effort. We have been self-sufficient for most of our existence. It has only been a very brief span of time since we decided to take convenience and dependence over self-reliance. The pioneers didn't have that choice. Neolithic man didn't have that option. It was either you grow, hunt and preserve enough food to survive, or you starve.

This kind of radical personal responsibility will put you back into nature where you belong and it will impact your overall wellbeing and physical fitness level. This will help impact your daily stress level and beat back that sedentary lifestyle.

As time goes on you will start to see a decrease in your monthly cost of living and your diet will change, too, if you are gardening and raising food.

There is something about off grid self-reliant living that speaks to the human being. This is almost a spiritual bene-fit. The work and the reward heal the human animal within you.

OFF GRID MINDSET

Off grid living takes work. Let's start with that.

This is by no means an easy lifestyle, but it is simple. If you don't feed the goats, they are not going to give you as much milk. If you don't lock up the chickens, then they are going to get eaten by predators. There are no games on the homestead. It's all amazingly simple and very cut and dry. However, it takes work.

People with a strong mindset for off grid living are those who like to stay busy. They are people who enjoy caring for other living things. You have to get rewards from doing all these things if you are going to develop or take advantage of an off grid mindset.

Days start early and end when you are done. There are surprises that might keep you up late. If you can enjoy the payoff of freedom and a disconnect from the system, well, it's all worth it. You really hold your destiny in your own two hands. That is one of the most rewarding parts of all this. If you do the work, you get the reward. If you choose not to, then you have to suffer the consequence. In a convoluted world where taxing happens, money is printed and divided up in ways that make no sense, well, it's nice to make it on your own.

. . .

One of the hardest parts of developing your Off Grid Mindset is to rid yourself of the dependence on convenience. You will be making the things you need rather than buying them. You will become more comfortable with treats you make at home than the treats you seek out at a supermarket or a convenience store. You will use things up, reuse them, make them, remake them and use parts of them to make other things! You will eventually be divorced from your disposable lifestyle.

The ultimate off grid mindset is one of self-reliance and independence. It sits best with those who like the idea of serving themselves, those who are determined to make their own way, and most importantly those who gain deep satisfaction from a day's work and the rewards that come from it.

YOUR OFF GRID LIVING QUESTIONNAIRE

1. Do you have enough money?
2. Are your expectations realistic?
3. What will your main power source be?
4. What is your gardening and farming acumen?
5. Are you squeamish?
6. How much do you value sleeping in?
7. Where is your water coming from and is it safe?
8. What can you not live without?
9. What makes a home?

If you can answer these questions honestly and thought-fully, you will paint a picture of what off grid living might really look like to you.

3
___

WHERE TO START?

I put the phone down and smiled. It was a very different kind of smile. Since I was 18 years old, I had been paying on that credit card. I spent too much, and I was just scraping by to make those minimum payments. Then at 30 years old, over 10 years, I made the phone call and made the final payment. I made several calls that day and paid off all my credit card debt. I was one step closer to off grid living. One step closer to that unique kind of freedom!

.   .   .

Up until now, we have had a lot to think about. I am sure you have asked yourself many questions and probably discussed many things with your family. Those steps are especially important. If you have made it this far, well, now it is time to start acting. This is the chapter where the rubber meets the road.

Any off grid journey begins by getting LEAN. We have to become aware of our living expenses and do what it takes to cut them down to a bare minimum. You might have a little work to do to get expenses down or you might have a serious load, but either way, there is wiggle room. We are all spending far too much money on things we do not need.

Understanding where you are in all of this will require you to take a hard look at expenses and create a budget for off grid living. We are also going to look at homestead transitioning and the importance of doing that stuff now.

MONEY HIDDEN IN PLAIN SIGHT

When the pandemic restrictions closed our nearby gym, they offered us an online fitness option that was just $10 and you could take as many classes as you'd like. After a year we had used this online service about 5 times! Fitness is important to our family, so we make the trek to real gyms. We have workout equipment at home, but this service just did not cut it.

.   .   .

I spent $120 on this service before I remembered that I was still paying for it! I had forgotten all about it. This was a small bill but a bill nonetheless that I was paying every month by auto draft. Without checking my bank statements, I would have kept paying that $10 a month for another year!

Many of us are paying for things we rarely use and it's that easy to lose some of that money month over month and forget about that bill! It's wild how quickly these things can happen. They just happen! You sign up and tell yourself to cancel or you sign up and find out you don't need the service, but life gets busy. This happens to people all the time.

There is also the illusion of services that you do need. There are tons of services that Americans assume they NEED but either just enjoy rarely or even not at all. The best example of this is Amazon Prime. Do you really need 2 hour delivery? Does anyone even need guaranteed 2 day delivery? That is the question, right?

And what about our entertainment expenses? How many streaming services are you subscribed to? Do you even use your cable TV that you're paying for? Can you live with YouTube's 30 second ads instead of paying for them to be taken away?

How many of these services are you entirely overlooking? How many things are you paying for that you simply do not need? How hard would life be if you got rid of some of these monthly bills that make life a little easier or more convenient?

Once you have done some work to find all of that money hiding in plain sight, it's time to move on to your other expenses and create a budget that will work for you.

EXPENSES AND BUDGET

The ultimate goal is to find yourself living debt free on the off grid homestead. Depending on where you are in life will determine how easy or hard this is going to be. For someone carrying a lot of new debt and making little money, such is the case with most students, the off grid life might be a big challenge.

Someone further along in their career might have a decreasing debt load and there are big benefits to that! No matter what the situation is, it is time to look at your money and truly add up how much debt you have, how much money is flying out the door that you don't even know about or think about and how much money you have after it is all said and done, i.e., disposable income.

There is only one way to utterly understand how much disposable income you have and that is to create a budget. Many people operate some form of simple budget in their heads. You know you are making a certain amount of money and it has to pay for a certain amount of bills or else bad things start to happen, right? Simple budget.

What you need to do is sit down with all parties that are going to be involved with this transition off grid and tally up all the income and all the expenditures. Get your bank statements. Go line by line for a month or two and see where your money is going. Pay close attention to that withdrawals column!

These kinds of deep dives often expose some serious things. This can be in the form of a revelation of expenditures on your end! In other words, you might find out that you are dropping over $100 a week on coffee and lunch! That is a serious expenditure that can easily be curbed.

This is also a better way of finding that money that is hidden in plain sight. You might see some charges on your bank statements that you are not sure about. It helps to give yourself time to look these things over and call your bank if you have any questions. In this day and age, it is quite common to be paying for something you signed up for 5 years ago! Now, it's nothing but a drain on your monthly resources.

Once you establish how much money you are spending and how much you have left over, you can start to manipulate that monthly budget and trim away at that which is not necessary. From here, you can take on these bigger picture debts. Money from monthly subscription services can be repurposed to pay off debt.

If you are looking for a quicker means of paying down debt and getting on with this move ASAP, you might consider an endurance year. While most people are looking to take a GAP year, some off grid homesteaders that I know took what I affectionately call an Endurance Year.

AN ENDURANCE YEAR

Our first year on our off grid property was spent living in a short trailer. It was tight living, and it was minimalist living for a full year. We put everything we had in storage but for a few essentials and we worked our butts off! We ate cheap and we lived cheap, and we did so on a limited budget.

Of course, we had no mortgage and we had little overhead. We were off grid in our tiny trailer, but it was a struggle. I call this the endurance year and the truth is, there are lots of people who have stories just like this one! People I know who have made the jump to off grid living or even just rural living have done so by having some version of an endurance year.

I know one man who told his wife, "I am going to work every Saturday this year!" His endurance year netted him 10's of thousands of more dollars by putting in the work and he was able to turn that into an opportunity.

.   .   .

Another couple, close to us, lived a year in exactly the same way we did before breaking ground on a home on their land. They are now living on 40+ acres in western North Carolina and they have pigs, grapes, gardens and even a little gas station where they stock up on fuel!

An older couple made the jump from suburban life to rural life in the Ozarks and they too stayed in a tiny home for a little over a year. They expanded on that home, but they certainly faced their own challenges being 100% off grid. Each year they add a little more to their operation up there. It's admirable.

Most regular people have the endurance year. I will be clear and tell you that this is a year that really sucks. It's a brutal year that tests you and everyone in your family. However, it is also a year that tends to dissolve over time. When you are years down the line, you will come to recognize this as a year you enjoy thinking of rather than one that you despise. The struggle of it all is replaced by fond memories and a sense of serious accomplishment. Whenever we struggle for something and achieve it, we are truly reaching the pinnacle of what it means to be human.

Don't be afraid of taking on an endurance year. You will learn and grow so much. This might be the perfect opportunity to pay down debt or just stock up on money for your new off grid home. Whether you do your endurance year in a trailer or from your current home and just stack money, it's something worth considering.

THE IMPORTANCE OF HOMESTEAD TRANSITIONING

While you might not be financially prepared to begin the off grid lifestyle, now is the time when you can start doing all kinds of homesteading things where you live. There is no point in waiting till you get to your homestead to start gardening, using solar power and experimenting with things like compost. Why wait? We have to live in the now, no matter what the situation.

Something as simple as building a rain barrel and installing it can give you a whole new outlook. It's part of that transition. Keeping chickens, even in an urban setting, is something that you can do! You might only be able to keep 6 or so, but it is experience.

You might not like the idea of a micro orchard in your backyard. It's easy to think that growing 5-6 fruit trees is just not the size and scope of what you want to do on your homestead property. Plus, you are going to invest in a property you plan to leave. However, you are going to learn important skills like nursing young trees to health, fertilizing and pruning. You will come to know the bugs and diseases that can affect different kinds of fruit trees.

When you crash land on your off grid property you will already have this skill in your back pocket.

. . .

You are an off grid homesteader now. You just aren't living on your off grid homestead. That is the mentality that you need to keep. That is the mentality going forward. Start ambitious projects and start learning new skills.

Remember that adding chickens, trees and beautiful gardens to your current home or property is only going to make it more appealing to most people. The money you make from selling your home could play a huge role in getting you out of debt completely or further carrying much less debt. This is a huge consideration.

Live as though you are an off grid homesteader, starting today. Don't make the mistake of waiting till you arrive at your off grid home to start learning and doing things. You will just be creating a big gap.

This will also allow you to make big mistakes on a small scale. If you lose a flock of 6 chickens because of a faulty coop door, that is way better than losing a flock of 60! If your garden dies off because you overwatered, well, better to lose a few raised beds in suburbia than losing the garden that was supposed to fill your pantry with tomato sauce and vegetables.

4

LOCATION

The first 20 years of my life were spent just outside of Philadelphia, Pennsylvania. At the time it was the only life I knew, so everything about that tight row home living and radical outrage about sports and the general pace of life was normal.

. . .

Even though I grew up in a county with 500,000 people in it, I still sought out the wild, lonely places. My father dodged a bullet and started fishing around 30 years old. He found places like Chester Creek, Ridley Creek, and the Brandy-wine River. By the time I came to be he was 36 years old and had been fishing hard for years. He took me to the water, and I fell in love with fishing at a very young age. From about 7 to 13 years old I fished with my father every weekend in spring, summer and early fall.

This became the necessary yin to the yang of our lifestyle at home. We were loud, cynical, judgmental people from Philly. We hated when things took too long and made issues of things that really didn't matter. Looking back, it is astounding to consider how my life might have gone if I stayed there forever.

My beautiful wife was going to college in Pennsylvania, and we fell in love fast. When she told me she was from Rich-mond, Virginia I thought I could never leave but I sure didn't want her to leave either! Of course, living in the south was inevitable! Hahah. Now I look back and struggle to understand what I thought held me there in the crowded streets of Philadelphia.

This is a lesson in LOCATION. There is no research that will serve you better than the research on your off grid homestead's location. The right location for YOU is going to be a combination of many factors. There is no pre-ordained location that fits all people. As with most things, it's going to come down to what you want to achieve as a modern off grid pioneer.

LOCATION FACTORS TO CONSIDER

- Climate
- Energy Generation
- Water
- Taxes
- Prices
- Local Government
- Community

All of these factors are going to have an effect on what you are able to pull off at your new off grid home. If you decide to live in a coastal region or a plains region then you are going to have a huge advantage in wind power over living in a valley.

Climate may be one of the biggest factors to consider because you can really "hack" the off grid living effort in the right climate. If you find yourself living in a zone 8-10 location, then you are going to be worrying much less about things like warming your home in the winter months. You are going to have a much warmer climate and a longer growing season to feed yourself and your family.

. . .

There are places on the west coast that are basically beautiful all year long. These are places that you don't need to rely on much heating or cooling at all! So, you could find yourself living off grid and avoiding two of the greatest energy drains of your whole operation in heating and cooling systems.

Some areas with very warm climates like the southwest have their benefits, too. However, you will be dealing with serious heat and a region where water access is less than ideal in all locations. You could plan to dig a deep water well but that can be pricey.

Choosing a location is going to be about what you want out of this lifestyle and what you are willing to do without. I really like to cut firewood and I love the crackle and pop of a nice fire. So, while it would certainly be easier to live in a warmer climate and be off grid, sometimes it's not about easy. It certainly is not just about easy for me.

Then, of course, there are the elements of finance and government. Those west coast locations are nice but they are super expensive and the taxes on them can be radically daunting. Price, local government and taxes are all things that you need to consider, too. If you don't think that local government plays a massive role in your off grid homestead, then you need only query permits and building.

. . .

Some states like Arkansas and Oklahoma will allow you to build structures on your property with almost no government interference. However, there are states and cities where you will need a permit to do most anything! Any addition to your property will have to go through HOA, local buildings codes and zoning, and you will have to pay for any permits.

You don't wanna build an off grid homestead in a place that requires a permit for changing out your shutters! If you plan on adding things like rain barrels and solar panels to your home, well, it could be a big pain in the butt to get all that taken care of if you are struggling with permit after permit.

Of course, this is your dream, so if you have your heart set on living a certain way in a certain place then I would not dare get in the way of those dreams. Just be prepared with plenty of extra income. Prepare for delays and intervention on the side of the local government if your dream is to live in one of these highly regulated states. It can be done; it just might get a little painful.

GET TO KNOW THE COMMUNITY

Our first home was a cozy, cheap apartment on the west side of Wilmington, Delaware. I think rent was about $550 and we had a washer and dryer in our apartment! I was about 19 years old and I thought we were stealing from the person who owned the property. It was great! For about a week.

. . .

We did not visit the complex at night or talk to anyone in the neighborhood before signing a lease. We just went with this big move and found ourselves living in a very dangerous part of town. It would just get worse and worse.

My car was broken into several times and we soon found out that no one would deliver a pizza or Chinese food to us after dark. We had a mouse infestation in the winter months. The final straw that broke the camel's back was when a shootout happened outside our apartment window and a young man was killed. That was the limit. We were out of there.

We learned a lot from this experience. We were young and dumb and trying to get out of our parent's house. We jumped before looking.

While you likely won't find yourself living the off grid life in the middle of a ghetto, you could put yourself or your mission at risk by not first getting to know the community you are moving into. Some rural communities are just not fond of outsiders. This can make life interesting, to say the least.

It's also good to live near a town of people with like-minded individuals. Having people of like mind is a big deal and it turns life into more of a joy. If you are going to take the time to truly build out this off grid dream, you might as well find the absolute best community for you.

. . .

You can visit these locations, or you can read about them in local news and even websites. If you are slick, then you can check around on Facebook or Nextdoor to find even more information about these communities.

WHERE TO FIND PROPERTIES FOR SALE

The first decision to make is whether you are going to be house hunting or land hunting. Are you going to build a home on raw land or are you going to buy a home that is already built and ready to take you in? Building materials and build times are way up in the nation right now. In other words, it is going to take some time for your home to be built on raw land.

Our friends, a family of four, bought a modest piece of land about 2 and a half months ago and began the building process. They are far from getting into that home. Our neighbors took the same path and found themselves living in a rental for what is going on 4 months and the building of the home has not yet even started!

This might not be your situation but it's one to consider. If you haven't realized this yet, the process of jumping off grid is only as enjoyable as you make it. It's a matter of doing some due diligence and understanding what you are walking into.

Whether you are looking for land or a home you should get a realtor or two to start the process for you. You can tell them exactly what you are looking for. Be sure you tell them EXACTLY! Get right down to the details of how many bathrooms, acres, square footage and so on. Let them know you are looking for a property that you will either make off grid or one that is already off grid.

Realtors have technology on their side, and they can basically plug your requests inside the database of properties and search each day. They will even send you a report on that search each day if you like! That means you get constant updates on new homes on the market and new pieces of land.

RAW LAND

If you are hunting for raw land, it might be worth looking for a local realtor who sells land exclusively. There are some things to consider when it comes to buying raw land. In the world of raw land, there is a whole bunch of jargon that you need to understand. There are steps beyond the buying of the land that might need to be taken. In short, depending on the plot you buy, there is a bit of a learning curve.

UTILITIES AND ROAD ACCESS

Yes, you are creating an off grid property, so you might be wondering about utilities. Well, the internet is a utility, right? Also, you might find that you don't mind having one aspect of on grid life available.

.   .   .

Access to utilities is also important if you ever plan on reselling the property. Maybe you find a great location and in the next 10 years that property value doubles or even triples! You might be ok starting a new off grid home somewhere else and selling that property. Of course, you cannot be sure another family is going to want to move in and pay for a home with no access to basic utilities.

Road access will save you money and make your piece of land much easier to work with. There are pieces of property out there that are literally locked by other properties and you cannot run a road to them! They might be cheap and beautiful, but you will not be able to leave!

TEST SOIL AND WATER

There is no getting back from this one. If you find that your soil and/or water are contaminated, then you have serious problems. This can happen pretty easily if you have something like a local mining operation.

In most cases, this means your well water will be contaminated and the soil on which you grow your food will be, too! These tests are so important, and they will make a huge difference in how much success you can have on your property.

If you get stuck on a property that has groundwater and soil contamination, well, you are going to pay out the nose to deal with it or you are going to be hauling in water and that is not how you want your off grid experience to start.

HAVE THE LAND SURVEYED

The only way to really understand your land is to have it surveyed. This will sure up your property lines, so you know what it is you are buying. Before you can build a home on raw land the land will need to be surveyed.

This process will also help you locate important things like utilities and easements on your land. That easement could be your access to road frontage, and we already spoke about how important that is.

Again, while the convenience of utilities might not be important to you, knowing where things like gas and water lines are can really help you avoid trouble. You do not want to be digging a root cellar and hit a gas line!

DON'T EXPECT TO GET A LOAN

Buying raw land is not the same as buying a home and most banks don't look at it that way either. It is pretty hard to get a loan on raw land. This is especially true if you don't have a substantial lump sum to put down.

You basically cannot get into a piece of land with zero down. Now, there are many raw land entrepreneurs who are selling through owner financing. This is an option that allows you to put significantly less money down and pay that land off over a 10 year period. This gives people access to this raw land quicker. Of course, you pay interest and are stuck with new debt over the next 10 years.

UNDERSTAND ZONING

How a piece of land is zoned will determine what can be done with it and on it. There are eight types of zoning and you are basically looking for land zoned in one way: Residential.

The other eight are likely going to be a detriment to you. If you are trying to build a home and keep animals on properties that are zoned as commercial, industrial, public, right of way, park or open space, then you will need to have that property rezoned, if that's possible.

You could find value in agricultural space and one perk of land zoned 'agricultural' is that you can get away with keeping animals even if you are not allowed to on land zoned 'residential' in the same area. Here are some different types of zoning categories you'll see:

- Multi Family
- Residential
- Commercial
- Industrial
- Public
- Park or Open Space
- Agriculture

- Right of Way

Zoning designations are not easy to change and are often baked into the county's plans for the future, so don't overlook this important aspect of finding the perfect area for your off grid home.

OTHER OFF GRID HOME CONSIDERATIONS

There is a growing LIFE OVER DEBT sentiment in our nation. Many people are forgoing college and traditional homeownership to have a life that is not chained to burdensome debt. It's a remarkably interesting option.

These people are finding that answer in mobile homes, RV and tiny house living. With a decent job and no debt, you can quickly amass enough money to buy a nontraditional home outright or with a small loan that is easy to pay off.

The appeal of not being burdened by debt for 30 years and student loan debt for even longer holds great appeal. As someone who is considering a nontraditional lifestyle, you might like the idea of living in a home like this that has very little overhead. You aren't dealing with the purchase of raw land or even the upkeep of a traditional brick and mortar home.

. . .

What better way to trim the cost of living down? If you are the type of person who could live in this style of home, you will see tremendous benefits from life in an RV or a tiny home. Of course, you forfeit the ability to have that big farmhouse, at least for now, but you will not have the mortgage of that farmhouse!

Some people are even living full-time on the road! They don't have a piece of property and instead spend their time bombing around the nation. This takes away the opportunity to flex those homesteading muscles, but it is an off the grid lifestyle that adds that kind of freedom to life.

FAMILY NEEDS AND PERSONAL SITUATIONS

Every family has its challenges. You might need to consider your location in terms of access to hospitals and doctors or maybe schools or other facilities that are necessary. Your family's needs are always going to be paramount and health issues don't just clear up because you decide to live an off grid lifestyle.

It's true there are numerous health benefits to this kind of life, but you have to be very careful about getting too far out and not taking care of yourself.

Prescription medications, therapy and other things might be hours away neglecting them would be extremely dangerous. You might also consider your distance from other family members. You could be in perfect health but your mother or someone important to you might not be. There is a good chance that you will have to make a trek to help them out from time to time. As time goes on, these treks might become more regular and could become a serious burden, so consider your family needs and personal situations when it comes to buying a property.

Where you decide to call home can have serious implications on your day to day life. That could be an on or off grid home. I have given you quite a bit to consider here from the traditional to the eccentric. You could find your off grid freedom on the porch of an old home in the country or in the bedroom of an RV parked at the base of the Rockies.

If you do decide to go brick and mortar, then this next chapter is going to be just the one you need to read. You will learn all about the various building methods that can be used and the permissions required. Don't assume that you have to build an A-Frame to live in. Have you ever heard of earthbag building? Well, your off grid homestead can be as unique as you like. We will discuss some methods in the next chapter.

5

BUILDING OPTIONS & PLANNING PERMISSION

I write as another means of making money off grid. It requires the internet and can be challenging at times but it's a side gig that pays. One article that sticks out in my head was when I was asked by a client to research and write about earthbag building. I had no idea what this was, but it sounded like something that would fall apart in a rainstorm!

. . .

It turns out that earth bag building is much more common than I thought and it's a pretty cool way to build a home that is not expensive but still really effective. I learned that earth bag building is a pretty climate conducive means of building. Most importantly, it opened my eyes to other means of building a home outside of the stick frame that most of us are accustomed to.

If you are going to live an alternative lifestyle like being untethered from the grid, well, you might as well consider some alternative building methods. In this chapter, we are going to go in depth on the building options and planning permissions that exist for the off grid homesteader. There are a lot more options out there than you might think.

Life off grid benefits most from this kind of alternate living because there are inherent benefits to these building methods. Many are taken from history when everyone lived off grid by default. Let's give them a look.

LOG CABINS

We're all familiar with these structures; there is nothing more romantic than the idea of building your own off grid cabin. Believe it or not, people are still building these things all over the place! Mostly, they are being built as prefabs, but many are being built in the traditional method, too! A well-constructed log cabin is something incredibly special.

Whether you execute a modern build or something that is more traditional, these log cabins have served as off grid homes for an awfully long time. Of course, quality insulation is going to be required and a nice wood stove might be worth the investment.

. . .

The log cabin is a great option for anyone building on raw land and looking to live off grid. There are many great builders at work across the nation. I would recommend getting one to either help you build your own home or to build it for you.

ADVANTAGES:

- The Beautiful Design
- Wilderness Feel
- Affordable

DISADVANTAGES:

- Specialty Build

COB STRUCTURES

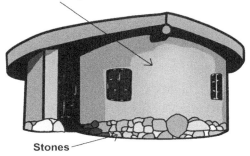

In the UK there are cob homes that are upwards of 500 years old and they are still being lived in to this day! So, as you come to realize what cob structures are, just understand that while it sounds primitive, it can be effective.

Now, to get right to the chase, a cob building is basically a home with walls made of straw and clay. The mud and clay are combined and then they are stomped down and compressed. This creates walls that are structurally sound. Again, while it sounds crazy to live in a clay and straw home, there are literally tens of thousands of people in the UK who are living in cob structures to this day.

In our list, you will run into structures like hay bale and earthbag that are less than traditional style housing. It takes a certain kind of person or family to give up life in a stick frame home to live in something like a cob structure.

If you have never been inside of a cob structure, I would highly recommend you visit a few and maybe even spend a night in one, AIRBNB style, before you consider building your home this way.

There are lots of courses on building this way. I would recommend taking at least one of these courses so you can do the maintenance on your home if something goes wrong. The technique is something you can learn and become proficient at.

This building method also lends itself to the creation of outbuildings on your property.

ADVANTAGES:

- Very Cheap
- Insects Do Not Eat Cob
- Cob is Fire Retardant

DISADVANTAGES:

- Permitting Trouble
- Long Build Times

TIMBER FRAME

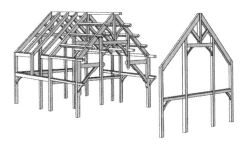

The Timber frame home is cost effective, energy efficient and often breathtakingly beautiful. It is really hard to understand why more people aren't building timber frame homes at the moment. Traditional homes have a lot of benefits, but when you walk into a timber frame home with the cathedral ceilings and exposed beams, it's something very special and very homey.

Timber frame is a style of building that uses whole timbers, rather than milled lumber, to join together the frame of the home. These timbers are cut in various sizes to create the frame and then joined together by wooden pegs.

These homes can be sided and insulated with traditional materials. They are built on traditional foundations, too! So, there is not a lot of unknown except when it comes to the frame style. Roofing is traditional, as well!

Timber frame homes are one of the best options for off grid living on this list because they really fit the lifestyle and they are very affordable to build yourself or to have built. These are serious homes that can give you the sense that you are living in a nice big open home yet a place that is warm and comforting.

ADVANTAGES:

- Aesthetically Pleasing
- Open Concept Stability
- Less Waste in Timber Frame Building

DISADVANTAGES:

- Vulnerability to Pests
- Swelling or Shrinkage of Wood

STRAW BALE

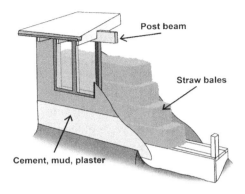

We all know the story of the three little pigs. After seeing what happened when the wolf huffed and puffed and tried to blow the house down, we learned that you do not wanna be the pig who builds his home from straw. I knew very little about straw bale construction but there are some incredible things worth mentioning when it comes to straw bale construction.

The first and most notable is the fact that a properly constructed straw bale home can last up to 100 years! These are not just bales of hay stacked on each other with a roof on top, the straw is used as a kind of insulated and is covered in a light frame and plaster on either side.

The other notable feature of a straw bale home is that the entire thing can be burned to the ground, and they were, when families moved away. This made them great options for pioneers who were picking up stakes and moving further west.

Whether you know it or not, nails were pretty precious, and the cost of nails could add up quickly, so construction methods that didn't require as many were valuable. In fact, nails were of such value that people would burn their house down in Virginia, sift through the ashes, put the nails in a box and then move! They'd burn the whole house down just for the nails!

I would certainly recommend visiting a straw built structure or building a straw bale outbuilding long before you decide to make one your home but either way, it's a building method that is affordable, off grid and pretty neat!

ADVANTAGES:

- Cheap Building Materials
- Good Insulation
- Sustainable Building Method

DISADVANTAGES:

- Harder to Get Insurance
- Susceptibility to Rot

ICF (INSULATED CONCRETE FORMS)

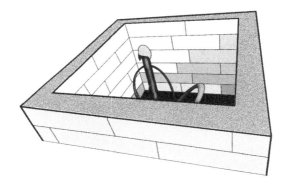

Insulated concrete forms are interesting building materials that are pretty fresh on the stage in comparison to other methods. The ICF looks like a kind of cinder block that has the cavities filled with insulation on one side. This is called rock wool.

Building homes using ICF is yet another innovative way that people are building homes and structures in the modern age. This is a green building material that is incredibly efficient in its production. There are lots of benefits not just to the off grid pioneer but also to the planet that we rely on.

. . .

People living in ICF homes and developments are incredibly happy with the structure and the energy efficiency. When you have a product that creates as little as 1% construction waste, that is a sticking point for many.

ADVANTAGES:

- Significant Energy Savings
- Severe Weather Resistance
- Faster Construction

DISADVANTAGES:

- Cost of Concrete Varies

YURT

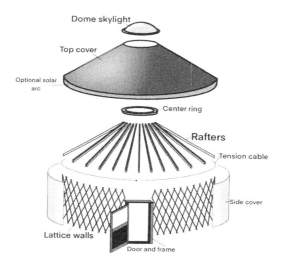

The yurt is an old school little home, yet exciting as well. It's become really popular with the younger generation, especially, and you'll see lots of them showing up on AIRBNB.

These homes are undoubtedly climate dependent. I would only recommend the yurt as a permanent structure if you were planning on living in a warmer climate.

As a shelter from the elements, the yurt can do a great job, but the extreme cold is going to get the best of you. You are either going to freeze or spend so much of your money on keeping the Yurt warm that it won't be worth it.

The yurts that are built today are either themselves round structures or panels that line up to create the circular structure. They are often given to lots of windows and a wide expanse inside. Of course, the yurt size is always going to come down to the cost. You can build your own yurt or buy the systems that are ready to build.

Traditionally, the yurt was a movable round tent. This was not a structure designed to live someone for the long term. The modern yurts are not really that either in most parts of the nation. If you were to face a serious windstorm it could take your entire yurt home with it, injuring you in the process.

However, if you are dead set on yurt living, you can get tie downs and modifications to yurts that will make things work a little better for you in severe conditions.

ADVANTAGES:

- Inexpensive to Build or Buy
- Cheap Utilities for Small Space Heating and Cooling
- Movable

DISADVANTAGES:

- Limited Design
- Bad in Severe Weather
- Shorter Lifespan

STICK FRAMING

This is your traditional home. The stick frame home is probably what you are living in now. These are reliable homes that are outfitted for a comfortable life. They can be easily transitioned into an off grid paradise.

Stick frame homes are out there on the market waiting to be bought. If you buy a raw piece of land, you can hire a builder to handle construction for you! All builders are very familiar with this style of home. You might struggle to find a company to come build your log cabin but getting a stick frame home built is pretty easy.

There are some delays in construction, even in traditional homes, as of late. So, building your own home with a contractor might take some time.

. . .

Whether you decide to buy a preowned home or build your own, this is a direct route to off grid homestead living. Repairs and other homeownership aspects are easy to deal with, too. However, this may not be the eccentric style of living that you are after.

ADVANTAGES:

- Many Builders Available
- Familiarity
- Appreciation Value
- Easy to Insulate

DISADVANTAGES:

- High Cost of Building Materials

RV OR TRAILER

The debt free movement has driven young people away from college and mortgage debt. Rather than start life as slaves to decades of debt they are doing things like freelancing and living in RVs. Not only is it more cost-effective, but it looks really appealing.

Off grid life in an RV probably gives you the most options when it comes to day to day life. You might opt to do away with the tract of land and homestead for a life on the road. Travel and homesteading really don't go hand in hand, but you can have an incredible time bombing around the nation in your paid off, off grid RV.

If you are not in love with the idea of building a massive homestead and producing lots of food, then you might like the idea of transient off grid living. You can outfit the roof of an RV with solar panels if you were wondering!

ADVANTAGES:

- Cheap to Buy
- Great Used Options
- Mobile

DISADVANTAGES:

- Waste Disposal
- No Land
- Hard to Grow Food

UNDERGROUND HOMES

Living underground is no new phenomenon. All throughout history, there were people who built structures in the ground and even whole subterranean cities like the city of Nushabad. People have sought life under or in ground for a number of reasons. There was a period of time about 13,000 years ago when the Earth's magnetic poles shifted and people had no chance but to seek shelter underground. It is said that lightning rained from the sky like a downpour!

Less exciting reasons to have a house that is built underground, to some degree, is to take advantage of the earth's ability to insulate your home. The dirt is a tremendous insulator and the deeper you go the better that insulation gets.

· · ·

Many homesteaders install a root cellar on their property. If you're in a subterranean home, you could add the root cellar yourself!

ADVANTAGES:

- Great Climate Control
- Incredibly Stable and Safe
- Environmentally Friendly

DISADVANTAGES:

- Constant Moisture Control
- Ventilation Needs

EARTH BAG

A popular primitive style of building uses what are called earth bags. We have been using earth, mud, sand, to build homes for thousands of years. Earthbag building uses modern materials to take these primitive methods of building structures and homes to the next level.

Earthbags are literal sandbags that can be filled with dirt and piled up to create the base of a home. The key to making earthbags work is to layer them in rows with barbed wire between each row. Think of the mortar between bricks. This keeps the bags steady.

Most earth bag style homes are built like domed structures, as it lends itself to the stacking process. However, I have seen earthbag homes in all shapes and sizes. Earthbag building is another great option when it comes to building underground structures like bunkers and root cellars. Living in an earthbag home off grid is like Hobbit status! Kind of a cool aspiration.

ADVANTAGES:

- Unique Shapes
- Cheap to Build
- Environmentally Friendly

DISADVANTAGES:

- Hard to Get Permitting
- Thick Heavy Walls are Limited in Use

PREFAB

Prefab or prefabricated homes used to carry around some stigma and in some places they still do. However, the prefab is a very cool way to live! Many of the high level finishes that people have come to expect in modern homes can be built right into prefab homes!

Prefabs are great for the off grid enthusiast. Most have one long continuous roof which is great for solar panels if you have good sun exposure.

Prefabs are built on I beams, and the crawl spaces are very easy to manage. These builds are much sturdier than in the past. They are also laid out much better. Most are open concepts that are great for enjoying the home. Most of all prefabs are much less expensive than traditional stick frame builds.

ADVANTAGES:

- Great Price
- Lots of Financing Options
- High Quality Construction

DISADVANTAGES:

- Tough to Resell
- Cost of Land

BOAT

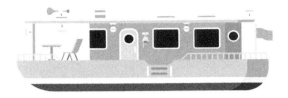

Off grid life on the water is another option. Houseboats and canal boats are incredible opportunities for you. These homes can range in price, but I have seen some really cool options for between $150,000 - $200,000. You may be able to get an even cheaper canal boat if you were interested in doing some work on it yourself. Life on the water is a pretty freeing experience, spending days on the water and returning only to resupply.

I don't think you would go about building your own houseboat from scratch, but you could renovate one.

Of course, you have to consider things like motion sickness and how life on the water might affect you. It would probably be wise to take up fishing as a means of eating out on the water. Solar power is another great investment when it comes to powering an off grid houseboat or at least the items on your boat.

. . .

Houseboat living has a lot to do with disposable income. You are not going to be able to get this done cheaply. In most cases, you will have to make an investment for a boat and for outfitting that boat with the things you need for off grid boat life.

ADVANTAGES:

- Beautiful Changing Scenery
- Less Expensive Than Traditional Homes
- No Property Taxes!

DISADVANTAGES:

- High Cost of Living
- Motion Sickness

HOW TO DEAL WITH PLANNING AND PERMISSION

The extent that you will have to deal with planning and permission for your builds will have a lot to do with where you decide to set up shop. Different states have different levels of involvement in the process. The goal is to live somewhere where the state mostly stays out of your business. Unless you are after a bunch of headaches.

There are some things, like homes, that are almost always going to require some permissions from the state; however, you shouldn't have to submit all kinds of permits and things to build a shed. So, do some research and keep that in mind.

Here are some great tips for helping you get over the planning and permissions process.

RULES AND REGS FIRST

Before you start anything in terms of planning and permission, you should get all the rules and regs in front of you. Spend some time learning them and get to a level of proficiency before you do anything.

I can guarantee you that this will save you some serious headaches in the long run. There is no point in submitting an application for something that you are not allowed to do, but you won't know that if you don't pay attention to the rules and regs.

APPLICATIONS AND FORMS

Take your time with the applications and do not be afraid to ask questions. Remember, you are now treading into the world of government nonsense. Things are slow, ineffective, and just an all-around pain in the ass.

What you might look at as a simple problem that could be solved with a phone call might turn into a few more forms!

Get someone on the phone if you have any questions about your applications and forms. Everything has to be done right or you are going to wait even longer.

Also, feel free to give them a poke if your application has been in for a long time without any movement. Again, things will suddenly start moving at the pace of government and that is rough.

OVER EXPLAIN EVERYTHING

When it comes to explaining your build, home, project, property, whatever, be sure that you go all the way overboard. If you are going to build a homestead and you are starting with a home, let them know what the future will hold.

You are submitting this because the government workers are extremely interested in what you are doing. You are doing this to assure that there are no surprises down the road. If you get through the process and find out planning and permissions has a problem with the large fence on your property, it is going to really suck.

Even though you tell them you are going to keep pigs on your property, that doesn't mean they are going to assume that will require a fence. In fact, they likely won't even concern themselves with anything but what you have written.

Be thorough and be complete. Better to have a bunch of projects on there that never come to fruition rather than several missing that become an issue.

GET INVOLVED IN THE COMMUNITY

Probably one of the best resources that you are going to have access to are the people who live and have built in that community. It is a great idea to get involved in the community that you are going to be building and living in.

Many of the people you get to know will have the real experience of building in your area. They will have gone through the process and they will be the most valuable asset in your toolkit. Get to know some business owners and people who might be living off grid like you.

BE PREPARED FOR INSPECTION

No matter what you are building, be it a home or a barn, be sure that your land and homesite are in great condition. Keep everything neat and orderly like you are expecting a visit. You see, this kind of mentality will assure that you make the kind of impression you want both during an inspection and with the community at large.

Be prepared for inspection at any time. Have a property that the local government wants to see flourish. One of the best ways to get local governments on your side is to make it known that you will be building a green home that generates its own energy.

In this next chapter, we will discuss generating renewable energy in its many forms.

6

GENERATING RENEWABLE ENERGY

This is a wild fact, but it is the best way for you to understand the amount of power the sun offers us each day. The amount of energy that our sun hits the earth within ONE hour is enough to power our entire planet for one YEAR!

. . .

So, it would only make sense to do your best to grab a little of that free energy raining down on us.

When it comes to generating renewable energy there are a couple of things that get in the way for the newcomer.

1. Learning curve for operation and installation
2. Startup costs

Renewable energy is going to be paramount for any off grid home in the modern age. You will have to be an incredibly unique individual to want to live the rest of your life by candlelight. You might be better for it, but I think it would be tough in this modern age.

STEP ONE: MINIMIZE POWER USAGE

Just as you have done with your budget, it is time to take a look at what you use power for in daily life. It's a guarantee that you are burning energy for no good reason with a variety of lights, devices and maybe even temperature control systems.

You can jump right into off grid living from the lifestyle you enjoy now but it is going to be a rude awakening. Having a successful transition to an off grid lifestyle is about building a staircase. It should not be about jumping off a cliff. The more planning you do, and the more transition work you do, the better off you will be in the long run.

. . .

The good news is you don't have to pull out the magnifying glass to find all the places you are losing energy on a regular basis. That is because we have a list of places that most of us are just wasting power.

The Alliance to Save Energy says there are 10 big energy wasting habits we should all pay attention to.

1. Leaving the Lights On
2. Using Incandescent Bulbs
3. Leaving Electronics In
4. Powering Empty Chest Freezers
5. Browsing the Refrigerator
6. Running the Dishwasher Half Full
7. Washing Clothes in Hot Water
8. Thermostat (too low; too high)
9. Not Changing Air Filters
10. Not Programming the Thermostat

Begin the process of whittling away at these problem areas. You will first see this in your power bill and you will reap the rewards when you start powering your home with things like wind, solar and propane power.

OFF GRID CLIMATE CONTROL

More than half of the energy that is used by the average household goes to heating and cooling the home. The best part is that most of the day homes are empty! That is why we mentioned programming the thermostat as a way to begin cutting down your energy wasting habits.

Now we can take that train of thought even further as we discuss a collection of ways that off grid pioneers have used to cool and heat their homes before the creation of conveniences like central air. We will also discuss a number of new methods and practices for affecting the temperature in your home.

HEATING

Heating is easier to do than cooling. There are many ways that you can heat your home using active and passive methods.

Fire

Cutting or buying firewood and using something like a wood stove to heat your home is one of the most popular ways of heating an off grid home. There are few off grid homesteads that do not rely on firewood to get through the winter.

.   .   .

Passive Solar Heat

Some homes are built to capture the sunlight through windows and sunrooms that subsequently heat parts of the home or help heat the entire home. This is a method you can use if you plan on building your own home. Be sure you take advantage of passive solar heat.

Essentially, you are turning parts of your home into a greenhouse. This will allow the sun's rays in through large windows and trap the heat behind the glass. This will require that you build your home so that the windows and sunrooms face the sun for maximum sunlight.

Solar Air Collector

This is an interesting method of solar heating. This method uses large blacked out boxes with glass tops to catch the sun's heat. These boxes have hoses that allow that air to escape into the home. Traditional home windows can easily be transformed into solar air collectors.

If you use passive solar heat, you can modify these areas to become massive solar air collectors, too!

COOLING

In most climates, cooling is a matter of comfort. In some it can be a matter of life and death, but the idea that you need to live in 69 degree temperatures all summer long is just not a good take for the average off grid homesteader.

While air conditioning is great, it is a massive power drain. When it comes to trimming away at the power you waste and getting lean for off grid life, most people either do away with the air conditioner or they find new and innovative ways to integrate cool air into the home.

The reality of cooling the air around us is that we have set up our homes to do it in a couple ways. The first is through air conditioning units that fit in our windows. The second is by running ducts through our home that blow cool air from a central air unit. That is the popular infrastructure.

Like many things in an alternative lifestyle, you will be introduced to methods of cooling that can be remarkably effective. So effective, in fact, that you might wonder why you hadn't done these things a long time ago!

Geo Cooling

The beautiful thing about the world underground is that it basically keeps a nice comfortable temperature no matter the time of the year. At about 6ft below the surface, you are going to get average temperatures between 50-70 degrees depending on the time of year.

Geo cooling works by driving that air up into the home. If you can pump 65 degree air up into the home during the summer, that is a system that is going to work for you.

By burying a series of pipes in the ground and having the air circulated up to your home, you can take advantage of this system in the winter and in the summer. Geo cooling is an incredible means of affecting the temperature in your home.

Fans

Fans are amazing because they don't use a ton of power, but they can really make a difference when it comes to cooling your home. Fans can be powered by a solar array; some are rechargeable, and some small ones can be plugged right into charged power banks.

It's worth the investment in power to own a few large oscillating fans.

. . .

Cheap Air Cooler

While I have never used one of these style coolers, I have seen good things about them. A cooler is filled with ice and a fan is installed either in the side or top of this cooler. The cooler is then used to blow the cold and evaporating ice water out into the room.

The temperature in that cooler is cold! When it's blown out into a hot home this method can make a big difference. Of course, you gotta have some ice.

Swamp Cooler

My father owns a swamp cooler or swamp fan. In the summer, when we sit on his porch, he puts some water in that cooler and it just blows over us. These are impressive tools for cooling.

The average air conditioning unit is going to run at about 5,000 watts. That is no easy pull and you do not want to have that kind of drain on your power system. One of these swamp coolers runs at about 600 watts and uses evaporating water to cool you.

SOLAR POWER

Remember what we said about the amount of solar energy that hits our planet each day? You have to harvest some of that if you are going to live off the grid. This can be on a solar array that is attached to your roof, or one that is laid out in your yard collecting sun. No matter where you place your panels, the process is all the same.

Solar panels are incredible. When the sun hits a solar panel, it literally creates an electric field. These black panels invite in the sun's rays which excite the electrons in the silicon cells.

This electricity is sent as DC (direct current) power through a conductive wire. This wire leads to an inverter. The inverter is responsible for turning the power from DC to AC, which is usable for your electronics.

. . .

From here the power can be used and stored. It can be wired to a breaker box that will power your home or to a collection of batteries that will hold the power for later use.

ADVANTAGES:

- Limitless power source
- Can be stored.
- Panels can be mounted in many places
- DIY and easy to fix

DISADVANTAGES:

- Overcast days significantly decrease power
- Large array is necessary to power your whole home

WIND POWER

A wind turbine works differently than a solar panel. Wind turbines are basically big generators. The wind hits the massive blades on these turbines and turns them. The friction in the generator creates electricity. It is one mighty idea.

Personally, I think wind power is in its infancy. The generators are going to get more efficient and the massive blades are going to disappear. This will create a method of power generation that is accessible to most.

After it is generated, wind power can be modified for immediate use on a large scale or it can be stored in batteries for smaller scale off grid home use. This power will need to go through an inverter in order to be usable in the home, just like solar power.

ADVANTAGES:

- Works on cloudy days
- Simple power generation to offset solar
- Doesn't require fuel

DISADVANTAGES:

- Large systems that are difficult to establish
- Wind is not consistent in most areas

HOWARD THOMAS

MICRO HYDRO POWER

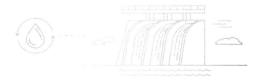

All my life I have been conscious of the water's power. I am a lifelong fisherman who has waded creeks and rivers all over this nation. I have felt the power of the water pull me and take me. I have seen rocks carved out by the relentless nature of water.

Water is yet another natural resource that offers up tremendous power, and yet so few of us take advantage of it.

The principle of Micro Hydro power is similar to what is accomplished by the wind turbine. Fundamentally, a turbine is spun; not by wind, but by water. These turbines are affixed in many ways. Some are under the water and others have blades that are turned by water that then turn the turbine.

·   ·   ·

94

As the turbine rotates, it creates electricity. At this point, the electricity is distributed in much the same way as the wind and solar power. This power will have to be inverted and stored in batteries that are sent directly to the home for immediate use.

Just as you need substantial winds to generate power, you will need a sizable body of water to generate power. Of course, not all of us have access to this.

The water should be flowing or else you will have to create a pump and power that pump. Flowing water is going to be your best option, but small creeks and streams will be very limited in the amount of power that can be generated.

For most off grid homesteads, you are going to use micro hydro power as a part of your entire power generation plan.

ADVANTAGES:

- Water is always running so power is always generating
- A great addition to other systems.
- Small scale systems are pretty cheap.

DISADVANTAGES:

- Most of the time it requires government intervention.

- Most people do not live on the kind of water that would power a home.

WHICH SYSTEM IS THE BEST FOR YOU?

When we were seeking out our own off grid homestead, I remember sitting on a small plot of about 3 acres. My kids were running in the yard and I was looking at a 100 year old farmhouse that basically needed to be rebuilt from the ground up.

The roof was a mess, the siding was a mess, the foundation and floors were all in need of being replaced. However, it was on 3 cleared acres and featured some incredible outbuildings. The land was awesome. I could see the solar panels lined up in the field. I could see the goats in another field. However, the home was just a wreck.

This place had those great cleared acres, and it was a perfect home to be powered by solar because of that.

The reality of choosing the best system is that you need to first understand where you are going to homestead.

I want to tell you another story.

Taking vacations as an off grid homesteader is a pretty rare situation. It is no easy feat to get someone to come and take care of your animals, your home and deal with the risk of what could go wrong. Most house sitters do not worry about things like loose goats or a coop that has been massacred by a predator.

If you find that house sitter, pay them well so they never go away! We found that great sitter, but we still call on them very rarely. We decided to take a trip to the coast. Our friends had told us for years that the Outer Banks in North Carolina were a wonderful place to visit.

The ocean is so close that you can see it from the road! It was a great vacation but what I remember most was the wind. In the Outer Banks, the wind blows almost constantly. Though I was meant to be relaxing at the beach, I couldn't help but think about wind power. A place like this would be perfect for a wind power system.

My point is that the type of power that you use is going to be unique to where you settle down. This is not only about the region in which you settle down, but the property that you choose, too!

Water on the property could be used to create micro hydro power. If you are in the middle of the woods with no cleared land, solar might not be your best option. If you live in a windy area, then you could take advantage of the wind power.

. . .

Ideally, you are not going to be on the lookout for an area that is the best for any one type of renewable power. The best move is to look for a property that can give you a piece of everything. Have some wind, have a creek or small river and have some cleared land so that you can gather that precious sun raining down on us.

When you have multiple power systems at work, it becomes easy to power up batteries and you worry less about off days. Suddenly, that overcast day is no longer the end of the world as you know it. Instead, it's just a day that might storm and bring high winds to power those turbines or rushing waters to the water turbines.

HOW BATTERY STORAGE AND INVERTERS WORK

There are many components to an off grid power system. It helps to become as familiar with these components before you start depending on renewable energy as your only means of keeping the lights on. This off grid power might be something to explore in your transition period.

A small solar array works off the same principles and uses many of the same components as a whole house system. So, when you start playing around on the micro it will help you better understand the macro.

Two components that everyone who aspires to get off grid should understand are battery storage and inverters.

. . .

To understand these things, you have to first understand the difference between DC and AC power. Direct current and alternating current are the two types of power that will make up your off grid power systems.

When electric power is created, through any number of methods, it is created in a form called direct current or DC power. This is power that is best used in short distances. It is best for powering batteries and fuel cells directly. Direct current is not what comes flowing into your home from large substations. However, on an off grid property, it will be how all of your electrical power is generated.

This is where your inverter comes in. The inverter is going to change your DC power to AC.

AC power or alternating current is safer to use over long distances. Our homes are powered by alternating current and it is recommended that you do the same. The voltage of AC power can be changed using a transformer which allows it to be spread around as needed.

The process is pretty simple. Your friction based alternators like hydro or wind power create direct current electricity. Even your solar panels will create direct current. As it is generated, the power will flow to your inverter and that inverter will change it from DC (short distance power that works best on batteries and fuel cells) to AC power which can be used to power your home.

BATTERY STORAGE

If your off grid power system does not have battery storage then you will only have power when it is actively being generated. That means when the sun goes down or is covered you will have no power, when the wind stops you will have no power and if the creek gets too shallow to affect your hydro system, then you will have no power. This is not a great way to live. So, you need to consider battery storage for all your electricity generation. This adds another layer to your systems, but it is one that you will appreciate.

Let's first talk about how the system works and then we will discuss the types of batteries that can be purchased and used.

One piece of equipment in our off grid power systems that we have not discussed is the charge controller. This is a small electrical box that can be programmed to dictate the voltage you want to distribute to a power source. These devices are incredibly useful, particularly when you are charging batteries.

GREEN POWER DIAGRAM

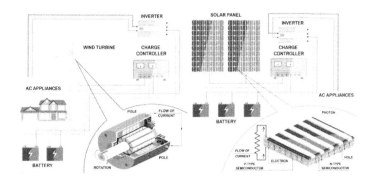

Remember, batteries can be charged using DC power. It is what they prefer. A good example of this is in your car. Your alternator creates a charge of DC power that is then sent directly to the battery to maintain its charge. You do not need an inverter for that. However, to avoid overpowering your batteries, your charge controller can send a specific charge to the lines that charge your batteries.

The charge controller can also send power directly to the inverter and into your home. This is power that is generated when conditions are right by wind, solar or hydro. In other words, when the sun is out, the power can be split to your home and batteries. When the wind stops and the sun goes behind the clouds, your battery system will kick in.

. . .

Battery power will flow back up through your charge controller. This will be DC power. It will then go through the inverter and be sent to your home for use. This is how you want your system to be managed so that you have power even when conditions for generating power are not at their best.

TYPES OF STORAGE BATTERIES

There are a variety of batteries that can be used to store power that is generated off grid. We are going to look at the most popular types of batteries on the market today. Each type has some pros and cons.

LEAD ACID

When it comes to storing power there is one battery type that has long reigned supreme and that is the lead acid battery. This is still the most widely used battery in solar power systems. If you are not sure what we mean by lead acid battery, just think of your car battery. Oftentimes solar systems are feeding rows of these lead acid batteries.

ADVANTAGES:

They are reliable and affordable and that is why people are still using them today.

DISADVANTAGES:

One of the biggest problems with lead acid batteries is that they only have a lifespan of about 5-10 years.

LITHIUM ION

Some of the most innovative technologies are being introduced using this newer technology, such as Elon Musk's
design for TESLA, the Powerwall Battery. LG also has a
product on the market called the Chem RESU. These
batteries can hold a lot of power in a small area and that is
what gives them their appeal for off grid home systems.

ADVANTAGES:

The lithium ion battery offers you a lot of benefits. It has a
longer lifespan than the lead acid battery (10 year warranty)
and doesn't require regular maintenance.

DISADVANTAGES:

Price is the big con when it comes to lithium ions. They are
expensive. The other issue is that they can catch fire easier
than lead acid batteries due to a condition called thermal
runaway. However, proper installation can basically negate
this problem.

NICKEL CADMIUM

These batteries are not nearly as popular as the previous ones that we mentioned. However, they are pretty popular in the aircraft industry. This is not a new technology, but it is one that could be considered for your off grid power system. These batteries are more ideal for larger utility solar systems.

ADVANTAGES:

Durability and weather extremes are two reasons to consider the Ni-Cd batteries.

DISADVANTAGES:

The biggest con when it comes to cadmium batteries is the fact that cadmium is incredibly toxic. The use of cadmium is banned in many nations because of this.

FLOW BATTERIES

The most innovative tech in the off grid energy storage right now is called flow battery. These large batteries use an electrolyte water mixture to carry charges between two chambers and hold a charge. What is most interesting about flow batteries is that they have 100% charge depth. In other words, you can use all the energy stored in that battery.

ADVANTAGES:

The 100% charge depth as well as the water in these batteries makes them fire retardant.

DISADVANTAGES:

To be frank, the technology is too expensive now and the batteries are too big to be a viable solution for residential locations at the moment. However, it is worth keeping an eye on this technology.

THE IMPORTANCE OF A GENERATOR BACK UP

In 2013, after a rash of power outages and system failures, I decided, even as an off grid homesteader, that we needed a backup generator. There is no one to call when your power goes out. There is no power company to report your outage to. Most importantly, there is nobody coming to fix your system.

That means if your system gets destroyed in a storm or if something important fails, well, you are out of power until

YOU get the part and YOU fix it. If the part is on backorder or if you need to learn how to fix it, well, you have no power.

A simple 5500 watt portable gas generator can power your important electronics. You can have things like refrigeration, small electronic climate control, lights, entertainment and the like. You can even power washers and dryers to keep up with washing clothes. Of courses, these things are going to burn through lots of gas over a few days, but they give you an option when the power goes out.

It is well worth the investment to get your hands on a 5500 watt portable generator. You can stock up on gas and a good generator for under $1000. It will likely be the best $1000 you spend because when disaster strikes, and it will, you will have a backup power system as your renewable power is coming back online.

TAKEAWAYS

The off grid power system doesn't have to be an over-whelming undertaking. You can use the sun, the wind and the water to power your home. Of course, minimizing your power needs will give you the most success when it comes to living off grid.

The single largest drain on your power systems is going to be climate control. If you can call on passive heating and cooling technologies to aid in that, then you will be saving serious power and removing the burden from your renewable power system.

Be sure you find out which of these renewable energies work best for you before investing in them. No point in buying up a hydropower system if you don't have any water on the property. What is probably the most important thing to consider in all this generation of power is safety. Remember, when you start creating enough electricity to power your home, well, you can also kill yourself with all of that so be sure you take precautions.

Now that we have talked about powering the off grid home, we need to have a conversation about powering the off grid family. One of the great benefits of living off grid is taking control of food production. When you start growing and producing food and preserving it, you are going to feel this incredible freedom rush over you.

In this next chapter, we are going to go deep on a variety of animals and food producing techniques that can be used to produce your own food off the grid. Even in small off grid homes on virtually no land, you can produce a lot of food. Hell, even in an apartment you can produce food!

From fruit trees to goats, this next chapter is going to cover it all. You might find that the idea of off grid living is but one passion and that the keeping of animals and growing of food is another passion of yours. Off grid homesteaders make a lot of money just selling their homegrown and preserved foods. Imagine that as an income stream.

Let's talk about powering the off grid family next.

7

RAISING LIVESTOCK & GROWING FOOD

I don't know if he remembers it or not, but my oldest son, when he was about 3 years old, posed for a picture in our kitchen holding our very first egg. We had nursed 6 chicks to adulthood and wound up with 4 roosters in the batch! So, on this day one of our two hens had gone into the coop and laid her first egg.

. . .

The conversation about chickens on the property was a couple years old. These chickens were our first foray into the world of producing food that wasn't plant based. We had some trees, and we had a garden, but we didn't have any kind of protein source like eggs.

When that picture was taken, my son had a little hat on, and he was standing proudly as he looked up at the camera. It's hard for me to remember exactly all that I was feeling at that moment, but I know that I had tremendous pride. I was proud that I could afford my son an experience that most children just don't have. Maybe more important than the experience was the connection to his food.

For most people, food is something that you go buy and bring to your home. There is a nearly mythical universe out there where all the food is produced and processed; it's just something that most people don't think about, either because they don't know or they just don't want to know. In just 100 years, our relationship with food has gone from seeing it in the dirt to having it presented to us perfect and washed.

The most beautiful thing about food production is that everyone loves it. Not only is it fun (and helpful!) to get your kids involved with feeding the animals and watering the plants, but it also teaches them valuable, lifelong skills through hands-on experience. Gardening and community gardening are both issues that are left untouched by politics as well. That is a beautiful thing and it's one of the rare bridges that we all can stand on in solidarity.

GROWING FOODS OFF GRID

The success you have growing food is almost directly related to how much effort you are willing to put into your property. I know several homesteaders in the Ozarks who have bought properties and dealt with abysmal conditions in the rocky topsoil on the plateau.

To grow in many places in the Ozarks, you are going to have to lay down about 4 inches of wood chips and allow them some time to begin to break down. When you add wood chips and other compostable materials in a mound to produce a high quality growing medium, it's called Hügelkultur. This is a highly effective means of creating nutrient dense soil that will nurture plants, flowers and even fruit and nut producing trees. It's a system that's been used in Germany and other parts of Eastern Europe for hundreds to thousands of years!

The point of the story is to help you understand that you can grow food in almost any place if you are determined.

So, what kinds of plants are you interested in growing?

ORCHARDS

About 5 years ago, we did two things that service our home-stead food production every year. The first was that we bought peach trees that were nothing more than sticks in the dirt. These trees have grown to be fruit producers year after year. We fertilize them and then we treat them for pests, too.

The second thing we did was recognize a native tree in our yard called the Paw Paw. Paw paws are amazing fruit producing trees that are native to the eastern wetlands as far north as Virginia. They are actually the northernmost trop-ical plant in the nation. The paw paw produces a big fruit with green skin. It's a smooth fruit that tastes like a cross between a mango and a banana.

We nurtured these native plants by destroying the competi-tion and weeding around them. For years now we have been harvesting paw paw fruits every September and it has been great to have these fruit bearing trees at our disposal.

Creating your own orchard can be a great way to produce lots of food without the labor intensive traditional garden. Some people love gardening, and some hate it. For those who hate it, invest in trees, and get yourself some kind of orchard. I really like the success we have had intermingling native and nonnative species.

.   .   .

Don't forget about growing some nuts for protein, too. Almond trees have been so well hybridized that they are perfect for many growing zones. An almond harvest is special and gives you access to a delicious food that can make every snack time a little healthier. Again, scour your property for native nut producing species. You might happen upon things like hickory nuts or black walnuts in areas near water. We have found hazelnuts on our little property and have done our best to nurture those small trees.

If you are going to have an orchard then you are going to need to know how to prune your trees. This is the action of paring back the branches, year after year, to assure that your tree is capable of supporting healthy fruit. Pruning is a bit of an art, but it is basically about ensuring your tree can get maximum nutrition to its fruit. It is also about ensuring that branches are short enough and strong enough to hold up the growing fruits.

STEPS FOR PLANTING A SAPLING

1. Place bare root saplings into a bucket of water for about 6 hours prior to planting.
2. Dig a hole that is about 3 times the size of the root ball. This will allow you to backfill the hole with compost or other nutrient dense growing medium. You can also modify the soil. We removed the clay soil and added more material to aerate the soil.
3. Look for any roots that are circling the root ball. These should be scored underneath if you have roots that are circling the root ball.
4. Find the primary root and bury it just below the soil line.
5. Add generous amounts of compost to fill the rest of the hole.
6. Cover the area around the tree with untreated mulch. Leave about an inch between the mulch and the bark of the tree. This is to keep waterlog from affecting the tree. The mulch will hold in precious moisture for the new roots.
7. Keep the sapling moist by watering deep and often through the summer months.
8. Protect the saplings by surrounding them with some chicken wire or fence to ward off things like rabbits, squirrels or other animals that might destroy the young tree.

GARDENING

There are so many methods of gardening that it can make your head spin! You can grow food in a number of ways with a number of methods. There is a good chance that you will try your hand at several of these. In fact, you might use multiple methods.

We grow some food in pots, some in raised beds and even some in tires! It helps to be a little creative and very resilient. Gardens and parts of gardens are not always successful year after year. Sometimes the garden doesn't work. It could be weather, pests or error on your part. Just keep hammering and you will get a little better every year.

START WITH SUN AND SOIL

In my early days I got all tangled up in the variety of ways that you can create your garden. The varying gardening methods had me under a trance, and I could not get enough of them. I found myself building and shaping, all the while losing plants year over year.

It's common to come out of the starting gate on fire and miss the two biggest parts of gardening:

1. Sun
2. Soil

Without the sun your garden will never succeed.

If you hear nothing else in this chapter, please hear that. The thought of all the time, money and effort that I have spent trying to make plants that love sun grow in areas where they don't get a solid 6-8 hours of direct sunlight is depressing at best.

It doesn't matter how well you water them, weed them or fertilize them. They have to have the sun requirements met. It is how they make food. Imagine if you were trying to become a bodybuilder but you could only eat one small meal per day. That would never work. When plants are starved for sunlight, they are in the same boat.

Map your backyard for sunlight by watching how the sun hits your yard throughout the day. Note or map where the sun is most of the day and the places that get that big window of sunlight, that is your garden!

If you are on a heavily forested off grid property you may need to clear some tall trees to have an effective garden. If you go this route, be sure you consider turning those trees into wood chips. Nothing sets the tone in a garden like a nice bed of wood chips. Of course, that brings us to our next topic and the second most important part of any garden. Soil.

SOIL

Great soil for growing food does not come in a bag. It comes from a process. The natural process of organic matter falling dead and decomposing on the soil, the natural process of earthworms and other bugs boring through the soil to aerate it and of course the microbiology and mycelium that break down components in the soil for easy absorption by your plants.

Great soil is a living, breathing collection of organisms that are symbiotic in nature and share that relationship with the things you plant in your garden.

Of course, there is another aspect to your soil, too. That is the pH. Acidic soil will support some plants and alkaline soil will support others. You can affect the pH in your soil to make alkaline soil more acidic and vice versa. Of course, you cannot affect anything properly until you test your soil.

Most people avoid the simple pH test for their soil and it's really silly. Test kits can be bought at garden centers and hardware stores all over the place. They are cheap and will help you to understand what will grow best in your soil.

Plants for Acidic Soil

- Carrots
- Cauliflower
- Sweet Potatoes
- Pumpkin
- Pepper
- Radish
- Garlic
- Eggplant
- Rhubarb
- Tomato
- Turnip
- Cucumber

Plants for Alkaline Soil

- Asparagus
- Beets
- Beans
- Greens
- Lettuce
- Spinach
- Cilantro
- Celery
- Brussels Sprouts
- Composting

You can affect the pH of your soil by adding amendments. You can affect every aspect of your soil, in fact, by adding the right things. Some soils are clay based and compacted, they often need things like sand, coconut coir and compost added to them to aerate the soil and give your roots some breathing room.

Amendments like Peat moss, gypsum and lime can all affect your soil's pH. This is why raised bed gardening is so popular because you can build your beds and then you can build your soil from scratch to fit whatever is going to be grown in that raised bed.

Once you have hammered down the best area on your property for maximum sun and you have learned about your soil, it is time to start considering what methods you are going to use to grow food.

RAISED BEDS

There are many reasons to start a raised bed garden. Along with being able to manipulate the growing medium, you can also create a beautiful aesthetic. Raised beds keep your plants off the ground and raised above dogs or backyard animals that might otherwise trample them.

While the popular method of building raised beds is using lumber, you can use all kinds of materials to create a raised bed. I have created them from wood, plastic prebuilds, cement blocks, pallets, stones, blocks and wood combinations. I have even made raised beds from rounds of wood lined up to create a bed. These decompose and create great soil, too!

The raised bed is such a great method of growing. It is one of the most protective means of growing food as you can put space between your food and the kids or creatures that run in the yard. I have had the majority of my gardening success in raised beds.

HÜGELKULTUR

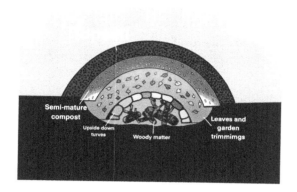

Semi-mature compost

Upside down turves

Woody matter

Leaves and garden trimmimgs

This could be the best method of transforming land into quality land for growing food. Sometimes, you just have to make it. You have to take your dustbowl or your rocky hillside and transform it into a pristine growing opportunity.

Hügelkultur basically mimics nature's method of making great soil for growing things. If you head into the forest and pay attention to what nature is up to, you will quickly understand the process of hügelkultur.

The rich forest floor is made up of decayed wood, leaves and dead grasses and plants. In hügelkultur you are mimicking that process. Traditionally, you create a mound that begins with sticks and wood. That mound is covered by leaves and dead grasses, this is then covered by a layer of half decomposed compost and then a final layer of topsoil for planting.

. . .

As the season goes on, the materials beneath the topsoil will break down and feed your plants. At the end of the year, you are going to have some quality soil that can be added to next year. This process can turn almost any kind of soil into something you can grow food in.

Here is the hügelkultur layering in order.

1. Wood Chips and Sticks
2. Leaves and Grass
3. Half-Decayed Compost
4. Topsoil for Growing

PERMACULTURE

To understand permaculture, you first have to understand the difference between perennials and annuals. If you don't know the difference, then permaculture is going to sound like magic. In fact, it might sound like magic anyway.

Annual Plants – When these plants die after the first frost of the year, they will not return the following spring. Things like tomatoes, peppers and cucumbers are all annuals.

Perennial Plants – These plants will return in spring even after dying through winter. Plants like asparagus, blackberries, sunchokes and strawberries are all examples of perennial plants.

Permaculture is the process of recreating the natural landscape of a forest in order to have your plants and trees become, basically, self-sustaining. In short, you will have a collection of food producing plants that return year after year and require little upkeep.

This process comes by creating your own little microhabitats. These small groups of trees and plants all work together to help each other. It is an astounding symbiosis that will also produce food for you and your family!

. . .

These little microhabitats are created in concentric circles with a fruit or nut tree at the heart of them. A few vining perennials can be added to these trees (grapes, hearty kiwi) to climb these trees. A couple vining plants will work with your trees rather than choke them out.

Outside of the vining plants, you can add fruiting bushes like blueberries that encircle the tree. Maybe 4 plants with one on each side. You can add beneficial ground cover to this area, too! All of these things work together in symbiosis.

The area can be bolstered with other types of bushes, medicinal plants or even flowering bushes to bring pollinators. Either way, you are creating small food forests that are beneficial to the world around you and your family. Best of all, these plants are perennial and they will be back year over year to produce more food!

Permaculture is an amazing opportunity for your off grid property.

HYDROPONICS AND AQUAPONICS

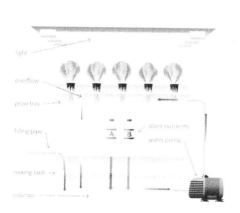

Up until now, we have been focusing on soil and the natural processes of growing. We are now going to jump from the soil to another growing medium, hydroponics and aquaponics. This is a method of growing food in nutrient-rich water that is incredibly efficient and has a profound effect on the speed of growing food.

One of the most interesting things about hydroponics is that with flowing water that has a balanced pH and nutrients in the water, you can even grow food inside with grow lights! Imagine growing food in your home and outside!

· · ·

Of course, hydroponics does better under the natural sun but there is something to be said about being able to grow food all year round in a hydroponics system.

Hydroponic foods are full of nutrients and grow larger quicker than plants that grow in the dirt! That is because you control so much about the process and there is almost no unknown. You will not do battle with pests or any kind of disease that is born of the soil in a hydroponics system.

The downside of growing food in one of these water based systems is that you have to buy nutrient drops to add to the soil to keep it at its best. So, unlike your permaculture system, it will not be such a hands-off means of growing food.

These systems can be created using PVC and some water pumps. It is not hard to build your own hydroponics system. However, this system has become extremely popular so you can even buy kits that are pre-made. These are also very affordable because the system itself is pretty easy to manage.

Symbiotic relationships are all around us and when it comes to growing food, they are very important. Another such relationship exists in aquaponics. Now, aquaponics uses the hydroponics system but adds another layer. Aquaponics is the process of raising fish in a tank that is below your hydroponics system.

. . .

If you can understand and operate an aquaponics system, well, you can not only grow plants, but you can also raise fish like bass, tilapia or even trout, in the right conditions.

You can grow plants like duckweed to feed your fish or you can create a black soldier fly farm to feed them. You could also just buy fish pellets. The two we first mentioned are systems that replenish themselves. Your fish will eat, and they will empty their waste out into the water filling the tank. This will actually feed the plants that you are growing!

That might sound disgusting, but it works really well. Fish poop water covering the roots of your lettuce might turn your stomach, but I assure you, the taste, and the size of the lettuce, as well as the safety of this process, are nothing to worry about.

In fact, these can become self-sustaining systems that provide you with fish and food. On a large scale, you can have more fish and more plants than you might ever know what to do with. This is a great position to be in because then you can start thinking about preservation or selling the excess.

While it might sound complicated, you are basically operating a large fish tank with a pump and filter that is feeding the plants you are growing. You will need sunlight or some kind of UV light indoors. No matter how you build it, aquaponics is awesome.

. . .

Both aqua and hydroponics are amazing technologies that have been around for a while. They are alternative means of feeding yourself and your family on the off grid homestead.

RAISING ANIMALS OFF GRID

What kinds of animals will do best on an off grid homestead?

The biggest thing that will get in your way when it comes to keeping animals is going to be space. If you decide to go full urban off grid homestead, then your city will also become a big obstacle for you. However, the keeping of animals is easier and more rewarding than most people think.

CHICKENS

These are the best starter for anyone who has never kept animals for the process of food production. You can keep chickens as meat birds. These birds will be grown to a certain size and then butchered. Of course, you need someone in your home who is willing to do the butchering. That is the reality. It's not easy for everyone to just jump into the executioner role.

Don't fret! If the thought of killing chickens makes you woozy, well, you can raise them with the implicit goal of laying eggs! Eggs are such an incredible food, and a small flock of hens can just overwhelm you with eggs. They can produce up to one egg per day. So, having 12 chickens means that you could find nearly a dozen eggs in your laying boxes each day!

Laying hens can quickly become a source of income if you want to sell the eggs at a market or people around you. A flock of 2-3 dozen hens is pretty easy to manage with the right coop or coops and a good collection of laying boxes.

How you protect, clean, and feed your chickens are really the only pain points. Cleaning a chicken coop is usually pretty simple and can take 10-20 minutes depending on the size of the coop. They like bedding on the floor of the coop and in the laying boxes. Chickens also really like roosting poles to cling on to at night. These can be wooden dowels, or you can just go cut down some straight branches from a tree that are about 2 inches in diameter.

Having a clean coop is important but so is a secure coop. You see, chicken is delicious. We are not the only creatures who have it on the menu. Foxes, coyotes, opossums, raccoons and even birds of prey will try and eat your birds. Most of the activity takes place at night but you have to be fully aware that the protection of your birds is essential.

A sturdy coop that closes up completely at night with strong wiring and durable materials is essential. You will be incredibly surprised at what the creatures of the world are capable of when they are hungry. Chickens have taught me more about the resilience and ingenuity of wild animals than any of my personal experiences with them, and I have been an outdoorsman my whole life!

How your chickens eat is also something you need to consider. You could stock up on feeding pellets or crumbed feed and drop that into the feeder each day. Your chickens will survive this way. You can mix up their diet a bit more and provide them with food scraps. Many people keep their chickens in a tractor, or a movable cage, that keeps them safe during the day. This tractor can be moved from one patch of grass to another. They get to pluck seeds from grasses and eat bugs. This is much better.

We like to dance with the devil here on our homestead. We have an active presence of dogs and people around the yard daily. This tends to keep the predators at bay, so we allow our chickens to free range. This means they leave the coop in the morning and wander around the yard each day digging, eating bugs and mingling. They really love this life even if there is some risk. It makes for happy birds.

GOATS

Goats are my next pick for top homesteading animals. Goats are a lot of fun and they are milk and meat producing animals. Again, how much of that you participate in is up to you. Either way, goats are a cool animal that seems to fit in with the antics of an off grid homestead. They have a lot more personality than you think.

If you are settling on land that you want to clear of brush, well, having a small army of goats to set loose in that brush will make a huge difference. They turn your brush into food and then into milk! That is a pretty impressive trade off.

Small breeds like the African pygmy goat take up virtually no space in terms of building a barn, and they produce about ½ a gallon of milk each day! You could probably keep them in dog houses with doors if you really wanted to.

You will need goat feed even if you offer up the brush around your property. So, you may need to be close enough to a place where you can buy animal feed. For dairy goats, you are going to look for things like alfalfa, alfalfa pellets, grass hay and whole oats. Of course, they may need something like a mineral supplement and clean water.

Be sure you get more than one goat because they are animals that really love a companion or a group. Outside of that, your off grid homestead should have a few goats on it.

OTHER HOMESTEAD ANIMALS

While goats and chickens are our top picks for the home-stead, there are many other animals that are great to have down on the homestead—I haven't even mentioned dogs yet! Dogs are essential as companions, security and just a staple of the human home. They have been with us forever and there is good reason for it!

The following homestead animals are great producers and are worth managing. The off grid lifestyle tends to press you to consider the utility of things in your life. I think this comes from the minimalist mentality. You will be less apt to have pets and animals around that do not serve a purpose.

LAMB

Maybe you are not into goats. Well, lamb is delicious, and they provide you with something else: fiber! Now, fiber is an exciting thing that most people take for granted. The fiber community is made up of those who raise animals for fibers like wool or fur, people who process it into fiber and those who turn those fibers into clothing and other accessories.

The fiber community is growing and the making of clothing and other things with natural fibers is a great way to make some money from your homestead.

Even if you do not desire to get behind the loom, just having quality wool is a big deal!

Lambs are an easy animal to keep up with and you can even use goat infrastructure to keep them! That means you can give goats a try because they are cheap and easy and then move them out and move lambs in.

HONEY BEES

Keeping bees has become much more popular. This has a lot to do with the awareness of declining bee populations. The government was paying people to have beehives on their property and there is something to that!

While honey might come to mind when you think about keeping bees, there are also many other benefits to having bees. Have you ever considered the wax? Beeswax can be used for all sorts of things.

Bees are also master pollinators who will help you have success with your gardens and orchards.

Bees die. Whole hives can run away or get a disease and die off. You can make simple errors that kill your hive. That should not deter you. There are tons of resources out there for people who wish to keep bees. So, don't be afraid, these little pollinators can do great things on your homestead.

ZEBU CATTLE

Zebu cattle are smaller beef and milk producing cattle that can be kept in smaller spaces but will allow you to produce beef in the same way that a cow does! They will not need as much grass or space to graze and mature.

HORSE

Horses can become your homestead vehicle of choice! However, they are a more expensive and involved animal to keep than any that we have talked about until now. So, the infrastructure and the care for horses are much more involved than your goofy, fun loving goats.

PRESERVING FOOD

With all that gardening, growing, milking, and harvesting, you are going to find that you have more food than you need. Now, you can be a good neighbor and give all that food away, or you can learn to preserve foods.

Preservation will give you the ability to put up some of this food for the winter seasons or for when trouble besets you. Preservation is easy and has been long practiced by the human race all over the world! To be quite honest, it is more of something that we have forgotten rather than something that we need to create.

Canning

Canning is the process of using a hot water bath to preserve foods. Be incredibly careful with this process, follow recipes and use sanitized canning supplies. Improperly canned foods can make your family sick or worse.

Canning is a great way to preserve your food for a long time!

Drying

Whether we are talking about sun drying, freeze drying or dehydrating foods, it all works and it is a great means of preservation. Dehydrators can be bought or made. Fruits, herbs, and vegetables can be hung in the sun and dried.

Mylar bags or mason jars are great ways to store dried foods and as long as you keep them dry, they will last for a long time.

Salting

When it comes to meat preservation, there is something very special about salting and hanging it. You can salt and dry a ham in your shed using this method. You can cut meats in thin strips, salt them and dry them.

Even fish can be salted and dried.

TIGHT SPACES

Even if you are off grid in a tiny home in a small urban lot, you can raise food in tiny spaces. The important thing to remember is that complaints about animals are always going to be about noise and smell. They are also always going to come from neighbors. So, as long as you can keep some quiet animals and keep them clean, you will likely hear nothing from your neighbors.

Give them some of your homegrown food from time to time. Not sure if that is bribery, but you could just shelve it as being a good neighbor!

There are two animals that work better for this than any other. The first is rabbits. With a few males and a few females, you can let nature run its course and have a renewable food source that also creates compostable droppings you can add directly to your garden. Of course, you are going to have to off little bunnies and that is no fun.

. . .

You will need to have the infrastructure, rabbit pens, to support the growing population and you will need a food source for them, too. However, if you can handle these things, then you will be able to keep that population going strong.

The other species is quail. Quail are little quiet birds that lay eggs each day. You can keep 12 of them without issue and without noise in an exceedingly small space. Quail provide you with eggs and meat; that is what makes them so special. They are basically mini chickens.

Take advantage of these small space animals even if you aren't pressed for space. You can get a lot out of these little resources.

You, your animals and your plants are all going to need access to water. For the most part, you want that water to be clean and harvestable from a system that renews itself from time to time. This is why we are going to talk about harvesting water and the management of water resources in our next chapter.

8

WATER & WASTE

According to data gathered by UNICEF, every year over 85,000 children under the age of 15 die from waterborne illness. Water kills more kids than war! That's real! We lose 30,000 children of the same age range to conflict each year. This seems incredibly foreign to us because we are so used to having clean water.

. . .

The tap and our modern water system are some of our greatest defining factors in our success as a nation and the same is true for all advanced nations around the world.

Hopefully, this has made you aware of the importance of collecting and storing your own water supply. It will be especially important that you have a reliable system for your drinking water. You will need water to do much more than drink and that is important to take into account.

You are going to need about 3 gallons of water per member of your family per day. That might be an overestimate but trust me, you do not want to be in the 1 gallon of water per person per day camp if something goes wrong with your other water resources.

- Cooking
- Bathing
- Cleaning
- Watering Gardens
- Animals

WELL WATER

The most common water system on the off grid homestead is well water. When you bore into the ground you can find water, but this comes at a cost. Digging a well is not always cheap. It really depends on where the groundwater is.

- Cost of Digging Shallow Wells: $3,000
- Cost of Digging Deep Wells: $15,000+

HAVE YOUR WELL WATER TESTED BEFORE YOU START USING IT!

Most well systems are also going to require that you attach a filter to that water source. The groundwater might not be contaminated, but all water has some pathogens present. Also, well water can have a strange odor. You might also be dealing with something like hard water which needs treatment, too! Change your filters every 3-6 months.

Don't be put off by well water. It is about the only way you are going to get back to having a steady stream of water like the tap that you might already be accustomed to.

What you need to understand about your situation with water is where the water table is on a property. If the water table is close to the surface then you will have to dig less. If the water table is deep then you are going to need to dig a deep well and they are more costly.

WATER STORAGE

When it comes to storing water, there are some serious limitations that you have to be aware of. If your plan is to live off store bought water, you are going to do a lot of hauling of water. Water is heavy and it takes up a lot of space. It can be hard to find a good place to store all the water that your family will need.

WaterBricks are a product that can be purchased to store water from your well or rain catchment. Again, you got to have room for it. So, we use a number of methods for being prepared to meet our water needs.

RAIN CATCHMENT

Let's not forget that water comes dripping from the sky throughout the year. We can depend on rain catchment as a means of collecting water. This has been recently popularized by the use of rain barrels.

Rain barrels can be attached to your downspouts and collect large amounts of water for you and your family. We are talking about 55-60 gallons of water per barrel. Put those on 4 of our downspouts and you can see how quickly your water needs will be met during a rainstorm.

. . .

You could also look into cisterns that are attached to your downspouts and buried. These can hold up to 1000 gallons of water!

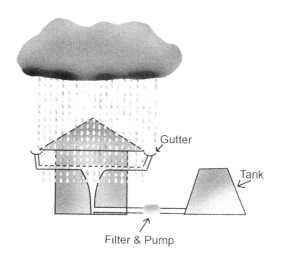

GREY WATER

The degree to which you need clean water is important to understand, too! Watering plants can become a huge waste of clean water. That is where grey water comes into play. You see, we use water all the time that hardly gets dirty and is completely safe for other uses. That is basically what grey water is.

This kind of water can be recycled, essentially. There are systems that can process your grey water from dishwashing and from laundry and make it safe to water your plants.

However, water from your bathtub or just washing hands and those kinds of activities can be used to water gardens and even for animals to drink!

Black water is another kind of used water that must be avoided. This is water that has been used to carry human waste. Black water is filled with bacteria from fecal particles and will make you and your animals sick if you try to use this kind of water for anything.

As you develop your water systems, you have to be sure that you are capable of separating the two. Grey water is gold while black water is illness. This is a pretty easy thing to do, and most homes already separate the two types of waste-water until they wind up in the sewer line.

Greencoast.org claims that up to 80% water usage in a household goes to grey water uses. That is a lot of water that can be captured and reused.

NATURAL SOURCES

Never forget about the lakes and rivers in your area. These are massive water resources. If you need to call on them in hard times, then you should have some kind of wheeled cart to assure that you can get the water from one place to the other.

. . .

A good map with all of these places marked on it will give you a resource in your time of need. Just be aware that hauling water from a lake is not always the most fun. However, it can be a water source when you need it.

WHICH IS BEST?

When it comes to water, we have our favorites down on the homestead, but the collection and storage of water should not be limited to any one option. This is a situation where you should take advantage of all the sources that you are lucky enough to have at your disposal. If that is the rain and a well, then use them to their max!

If you are storing water, pulling it from the ground, watering plants with creek water, well, use them all! With water, you want all the options. So, your off grid water goals should be to set up as many options for procuring and using water.

Gun to my head, I would tell you to spend the money and pipe a well into your off grid home first. That is the most consistent and reliable water supply that you can get your hands on if it's possible. The reality of digging wells is that you may not be able to dig one or you may not be able to afford to dig one right away if it is a deep water well.

Once you have your main water system in place, keep adding water sources to your system so that if something breaks or droughts dry up your well or creeks, you have extra stored water, rain catchment or other means of gathering water.

The management of water and hot water is one of the toughest changes for people new to off grid living. We take our water tap and hot water heaters for granted. If you can understand this and prepare for the change, you will have much greater success.

FILTERING AND SANITIZING WATER

Virtually every water source that you use is going to need to be filtered and sanitized. Remember, even your well will be filtered before it makes it into your pot or glass. Water has all kinds of pathogens in it. These things can make you and your family legitimately sick—remember the intro to this chapter.

When it comes to filtering and sanitizing water, the process is pretty simple. You are going to want a few things in your off grid home to make this process simple. We already talked about filters for your well water. Stock up on them. While they are effective and efficient, you are going to need to change them every 6 months unless you have lots of sediment or iron in the water, in which case you should change the filter every three months.

Having large scale filter systems is a great way to manage water resources in your home. Systems like the Big Berkey and other gravity drip filter systems are great options for this. You are looking for water filters that are effective against 99% of pathogens, viruses, and contaminants. There are a few brands out there that do this best. We are big fans of Katadyn.

Filtering not only removes harmful pathogens and sediments, but also the activated charcoal that is part of any high quality filter can affect the taste of the water. The taste of well water and collected water can sometimes be off-putting but filters can improve that taste.

If you are going to be gathering water from local water sources, you will want to also treat that water with some kind of Sani tab even beyond the filtering. You see, it's hard to know the full extent of contamination to long running sources of water. You can bet that animal fecal matter is flowing in that creek and river. Everything runs downhill!

These Sani tabs or other water sanitation methods are great for dealing with any contamination that gets through your water filters. The reality is that modern water filters are incredibly effective.

For emergencies, you could also store unscented bleach to sanitize water. If you have unscented bleach, you can use the 68/86 law to sanitize 1 gallon of water.

- **8 Drops of 6% Bleach to Sanitize One Gallon of Water**
- **6 Drops of 8% Bleach to Sanitize One Gallon of Water**

Finally, boiling water is the most effective means of dealing with contamination. This is the only way you can be 100% sure that all the bacteria in the water are killed.

TOOLS AND TECHNIQUES FOR MOVING WATER AND WASTE

Drainage on your property is essential both to the longevity of property and management of your water resources. How much water is flooding down the hill instead of hitting your rain barrels in a rainstorm? This is something worth contemplating.

You might also need to divert more water away from your property. This will preserve your foundation in the long term and assure you have a place to live on your property. The foundation of many structures can be washed out, molded or pest ridden if you leave standing water under the home.

One of the best and easiest ways to divert water is to dig a soak away. The soak away is just a few channels that lead to a larger hole that is backfilled with rock or pebbles. By creating a few soak away's on your property, you can divert a lot of water to the areas that you want.

HOW TO DIG A SOAKAWAY

1. Start by identifying the areas where you want to move water from. Where is the water pooling that is hurting your layout and property?
2. Then identify where you want the water to go. You should look for areas that are running downhill or away from a property. A soak away that is uphill from you will just fill up and spill back down on you.
3. Start by digging a few trenches that are no deeper than the spade you are digging. These 2-3 trenches will converge at a deeper hole, so assure you run them together where you want the water to end up.
4. Run a hose or dump some buckets of water down your trenches. This is an important step so you can see how effective your trenches are and if they will divert the water properly.
5. At the convergence of your trenches is where you begin to dig a deeper hole. This hole should be about 2 ½ to 3ft deep and 3 feet wide.
6. Add a layer of pea gravel to fill all of your trenches. You can add a layer of pea gravel to your hole, too. I like to add a larger rock to fill the rest of my larger hole in the soak way. Fill that hole up to the top and you will have a completed soak way.

One final point on the concept of managing water is the importance of having some PVC pipes, a few small water pumps and pipe cement. You could say that simple plumbing tools and rudimentary plumbing tools would also be beneficial because you can easily move water around the way you want. That's a big part of managing water.

Plumbing is a beneficial skill but there are other beneficial skills to the off grid homesteader. In this next chapter, we are going to go beyond water and plumbing to discuss a number of skills that are essential to off grid life.

SEPTIC TANK SYSTEMS

The term "septic" refers to the anaerobic bacterial environment that is created in the tank, this is what decomposes the waste.

A septic system is a very efficient self contained underground waste treatment solution. Wastewater flows from the home via the septic pipe, gas bending happens via the home vent or the optional venting in the pipe. Waste water enters the septic tank and the waste either floats or settles. Waste is then broken down by use of bacteria. Clear fluid is then discharged by gravity via the outward discharge pipe. The fluid is then evenly distributed to the drain field via the distribution field. Water is then percolated and purified by the earth until it is added to the ground water.

Septic Tank System

Inspection pipe   Inspection pipe

Manhole cover

Input baffle   Scum   Scum   Filter   Output baffle

Sewage enters from house

Wastewater   Wastewater   Wastewater goes to drain field

Sludge   Sludge

First compartment   Second compartment

To instal a septic tank system you will firstly need to instal a vent that connects to your toilet, this will allow air flow when you flush. Then you need to measure the appropriate size of your tank and dig a hole, allow for an extra 6-12 inches of space around the tank. Ensure you have dug the path for the connecting pipe. A tip to ensure smooth running water through the pipes is to have a 1 inch downward slope for every 4 ft of pipe.

You should then ensure the tank will not be sitting on any rocks, if rocks are present in the hole then cover the surface with sand. Carefully lower the tank into the centre and find a comfortable spot for the tank to sit. Now connect the pipes, making sure the tank is level but noting the direction of flow so the inward pipe is higher than the outward. Once the tank is connected and in place, fill the septic system with water. Lastly, fill the surrounding areas until the tank is covered, leaving only the top inspection pipes visible for you to keep up maintenance.

It is always important to contact your local authority and understand the laws and regulations you must abide by, before you start digging.

9

USEFUL OFF GRID SKILLS

One warm June day, my wife and kids approached me with a wrapped up box that had a bow on top. I could see the strain on the face of my youngest and the visual effort my wife was exerting to carry this small box.

It was early morning, but the family woke up early to surprise me with my Father's Day gift. Now, I have always been the type of guy that likes weird gifts, but this was one of the weirdest, for sure. I felt the weight of the box as it was transferred into my possession. Truth is, I already knew what it was.

Upon opening the wrapped package, I found a short length of train track that was cut from a larger piece of the railroad. I could see the flat bottom and the rounded top of the track where the train's wheels were supposed to run on. Now, I am no train aficionado nor am I some kind of enthusiast. However, this was exactly what I needed.

Months before, I had decided that I was going to start black-smithing. I wanted to learn how to manipulate metal around the homestead so I could both make some of the things we wanted and repair other things that we needed.

There are a host of skills that are pertinent to the off grid lifestyle. We are going to look at a bunch of skills that anyone living off grid can benefit from learning. From wood working to herbal medicine, there are a bunch of options out there.

WOOD WORKING

While woodworking is most often a lifelong pursuit, you can learn basic woodworking pretty easily. The value of a good book on the subject is immeasurable. Hard copy is best. Practice makes perfect when it comes to measuring and cutting wood. Practice simple builds to start, and you will find the areas where you struggle.

From building simple furniture for inside the home to building pens for animals, woodworking will give you the ability to modify your off grid property in any way you see fit! From here you could graduate to projects like outbuildings and maybe even build a new home on the property! The possibilities are endless.

BLACKSMITHING

One of the most prominent people in villages of old was the blacksmith. The ability to manipulate metal is a useful skill that allows you all kinds of opportunities. In off grid living, it gives you a number of options, the first of which is to repair things when they break or to recreate pieces that need to be fixed.

While blacksmithing does take some amount of strength and dedication, it's not as hard as it looks; there are lots of great books, guides, and YouTube videos out there on forging and blacksmithing. It might be an investment to obtain or build the right equipment, but this is a craft that is definitely worth learning on an off grid homestead.

I once made all new curtain rods through blacksmithing simple round steel into some arrow pointed ends on either side. The curtains could slip right over, and I had a rod that would never bend if someone accidentally pulled on them.

. . .

Making and selling simple blacksmith projects like S hooks can make you money at things like farmers markets or even online if you choose to go that route!

TREE REMOVAL

Really, the processing of wood from a tree to its most usable forms is a system you should become very efficient at. It will likely be the fact that wood fire is how you heat and cook most of the time. It is a great off grid fuel source and on the right piece of land you simply cannot run out of it!

Learning how to operate a chainsaw safely and effectively, a maul and an ax are going to be paramount in the success you have fueling your off grid home.

GRADING LAND

This is going to require equipment, but grading land is a great skill to have when you are working a new off grid property. If you can level land or slope land for your desired application, well, it can save you a lot of money.

I did not learn how to grade land and when we wanted to level off an area for another project, we had to spend money to have people and machines come out to help out with that process. It was never fun to pay that bill. This is a skill I wish I had learned before venturing off grid.

SIMPLE PLUMBING

As we mentioned in our chapter on water, the drainage and the movement of water from one area to the next are always important. Simple plumbing skills can go a long way. Also, the further out you are, the harder it will be to have a plumber come to your property without it costing you an arm and a leg!

Having PVC around and a good book on plumbing can make this easier. If you have the fittings you need, some PVC cement and a hacksaw to cut them to size, you can fix most problems in a simple water system.

COOKING

While this might sound elementary, being able to cook is a huge benefit to the off grid homesteader. Calling in lunch or heading out to eat at a restaurant could be an hour drive or, in terms of delivery, not an option. Knowing how to cook and what to cook is going to make life much better.

You should also become well-versed in cooking all parts of the animals you plan on raising; you don't want anything to go to waste! Also, learn to work with things like eggs and milk to create everything from cheeses to bread. This is something you can start practicing right now! During the pandemic, when everyone was stuck at home, yeast was off the shelves for months. Many people realized that they needed to get back to basics when it came to cooking, and bread-baking, especially, has made a huge comeback. If you want to really start from scratch, you can even get a hand mill for a few hundred bucks and make your own flour!

The one thing that stands out about people who excel in the off grid kitchen is their ability to cook from scratch and be innovative when it comes to the food they make.

CANDLE MAKING

Remember in Chapter 8 when I was talking to you about bees? Well, this is one of the most effective ways that you can take advantage of that beeswax that you harvest. Writing and drinking coffee by candlelight is a great way to start your day. Reading by candlelight is nice, too. It also saves that precious battery energy from your solar system.

Candle making is one of those timeless skills and people respect it. With all the harmful chemicals they're finding in mass-produced candles nowadays, homemade candles are becoming an increasingly popular alternative. It's easy to do, it's cheap, and it's another one of those things you can do to make some money on the side.

HERBAL MEDICINE

If you employ essential oils and a large herb garden, you can become something of a healer with herbal medicine. However, in order to become proficient in herbal medicine, you have to practice both the identification and the processing of plants. Essential oils are also great for creating stronger medicinal doses and helping with everyday challenges such as focus, sleep, and allergies (not to mention you can use them in your homemade candles and soaps).

There are all kinds of ailments that you can deal with by simply employing herbal remedies. Knowing the ins and outs of herbal medicine can be really helpful for you and your entire family, especially if the nearest doctor's office is a long distance away. A good book on herbal medicine is a must-have on the homestead.

SOAP MAKING

Now, we are talking about one of my guilty pleasures. You see, I have a weakness for high quality hand soaps. Nothing gets the day started right like a shower with a nice bar of lavender soap. Handmade bar soap is making a comeback, once more due to all the extra crud that's found in the manufactured stuff, and people love it.

Wood ash mixed with water is how you create lye. This is one of the most important ingredients in soap. From there, you can add all kinds of things to create your own custom made soaps.

HOMESCHOOLING

It was pretty common for people to teach their own children back in the day. The public school system is actually quite new. The gathering of materials and the creation of a class-room are essential for homeschooling. You might even be able to take care of other children close by if you have a big enough schoolhouse.

Homeschooling is not just a skill that you hone for yourself, but it will result in the education of your children and the way that they look at education in the future. Just imagine, you'll actually be in control of what and how your kids learn!

CRAFTING

While this may not seem like a skill you would need, it can be a great way to spend your time. You can take advantage of the natural world and turn your old grapevines into wreaths, corn husks into dolls and all sorts of things along these lines.

Crafting is great for off grid children and it's another way to take advantage of your abundant wildlife resources.

The great thing about all these skills is that they not only work to make your daily life better, but they also can make you some money! It is always good to have a few income streams on the off grid homestead. So, in the next chapter, we are going to get into just that. I think you will be surprised at just how industrious you can be while disconnected from the world, out in the middle of nowhere!

10

MAKING MONEY OFF GRID

A s a writer, the mornings start out much the same way. Most days I wake up around 4:30 in the morning. The amount of work in these morning hours is exponentially more than I get done in the afternoon. At this hour, the distractions are little more than crickets and the occasional hoot owl.

. . .

It's time for water and coffee, answering emails and organizing my day. I also try to take some time to be thoughtful and thankful for my position in life. I recognize that people have to get up and go to work each and every day. Many go to jobs they don't even like. It has been a long time since I lived that way, but the scars never seem to go away. I remember the dread of Sunday night like it was yesterday.

Once you open yourself up to this kind of life, all things become possible. By cutting your costs of living, you free up more time for new ventures. Living this unique lifestyle is also something that many people will admire, and they will want to learn and hear about it. You can monetize as much of your life as you like.

In this chapter, we are going to talk about making money while living off the grid. We will touch on traditional jobs and multi-faceted income streams that can all add up to a living wage and more time doing what you want in the places that you really want to be.

REMOTE 9-5

One of the great gifts of the pandemic and the rough year that was 2020 was the proof that many more Americans can do their 9-5 jobs remotely from the comforts of home. This is a paradigm shift in the workforce and in how businesses are run.

. . .

There will be more remote 9-5 jobs available as time goes on. For some industries, it just makes good business sense. The costs and risks attributed to packing a bunch of people into costly commercial real estate are things that owners and operators will be glad to see go away. Of course, not all jobs can be remote, but at least you know you can keep that 9-5, if you so desire it, with a steady paycheck.

Let's put it this way: the possibility of doing so is greater than ever. This will depend on what your skillset is and what you are willing to do.

Personally, I cannot imagine working a 9-5 while living off the grid. There is something about it that feels like a trick to me. After a while, you feel like living on the grid is a bit of a trap and then it seeps into how you make your living. In your journey, you start to develop things like radical ingenuity and radical freedom from old systems. After a while, it becomes really tough to consider answering to anyone.

That said, I know other homesteaders who just love having that check each week, the benefits and even the 401k! They sink some of that steady money back into the operations of the homestead and their reduced cost of living makes even a decent job feel like a real winner.

This is a very personal decision, as all of these will be. The next few are going to be centered around making your living on and with your homestead.

SELLING YOUR STORY

If you don't mind seeing your own face or name in print, there could be a huge market for you to tell your off grid story. YouTube Channels and blogs like The Prairie Homestead and The Elliott Homestead, or one of my favorites, All American Homestead, are great examples of how you can leverage your story to make money.

No matter how far along in this process you get, remember, you are taking a radical journey. According to Home Power Magazine, there are around 200,000 families living off grid in the United States. I do not know how many of those are in the lower 48, but it reduces the number further. Not only does that make your journey special, but it also makes it appealing to others.

People love the idea of casting aside their messy modern lives, tethered to wires and traffic, for something as serene as the off grid lifestyle.

From the moment you start looking at off grid properties, you can start telling your story in video, written form or both! Don't hesitate to capture the things that you find important. You could even create a podcast and discuss your journey with just a microphone.

So, how do you turn all of that into money? Well, there are a number of ways.

1. YouTube will pay you if you can get 1000 subscribers and 4,000 watch hours on your channel
2. You can get sponsors and advertisers through your blog, once you get traffic high enough
3. You can become a mentor or consultant to others who are going off grid
4. You can sell seeds and other useful items to people who watch and read you
5. Homesteading books can sell well for those with engaged audiences
6. You can even sell courses on the various things you do on the homestead.

Selling your story is often a money making method that takes a bit of ripening. It's rare that you jump right out of the gates into making money, but you can create a serious business over a few years if you get the right kind of audience watching your videos.

FARMING

This one comes pretty naturally if you are on an off grid property with space and start taking advantage of that land through farming and raising animals. In Chapter 8, we discussed this in detail. There are all kinds of animal and plant resources that you can harvest from your homestead.

. . .

If you plan for excess, then you will have things to sell at your local farmers markets or maybe even online. Shipping can be a big problem when it comes to fresh foods, so you have to be careful about what you get involved with. However, something like wax coated cheese can last a long time. Seeds are a great thing to sell, too!

If you can find a local farmer's market, then you can set up a table and display your goodies. You might even link up with the local restaurant scene to get your produce, milk, honey or whatever else you farm into local restaurants.

CSA boxes are another great way to leverage your produce and to get buy-in for what you produce each year. Now, this might be something you commit to after a few years of growing, but it is a better chunk of change and builds a great relationship with your long term customer base.

The CSA is simply community supported agriculture. This is a process where people buy shares from a farm. They buy shares of the year's harvest and those shares are delivered or picked up at a neutral location week over week or biweekly.

Simply put, a customer pays you for a few months' worth of produce, meat, and dairy in advance. Then you deliver that in some form of package or box on a regular basis. This is a very cool way for the customer base to support your off grid homestead directly. Rather than being paid by restaurants or depending on passersby at the farmer's market, you have people investing in your harvest.

Of course, you have to deliver that harvest or else you are going to have to pay everyone their money back. So, be sure that you know what you are doing on your land before you start selling shares for your own CSA package.

As you can see, there are many ways that you can farm and sell on your off grid homestead.

GOODS

Some of the skills we highlighted in the previous chapter can lend themselves to making goods that you can sell and make money from. Artisanal and craftsman inspired gifts are big right now and people like the idea of supporting smaller entities, as well.

Whether you start selling homemade wreaths or wooden furniture, or both, your handcrafted goods hold lots of appeal. If you can add a story to your work, then this can have an effect.

Each object is handcrafted on our off grid homestead in the hills of the Appalachian Mountains.

A simple message like this can go a long way to establish a bit of a brand along with your lovingly made goods.

- Crafts
- Soaps
- Salves
- Herbal Remedies
- Aged Cheeses
- Fiber
- Fabric
- Clothing

Here are a few examples of goods that you could sell both in person and online. These are all great options for any off grid homesteader who is looking to make some money through creative endeavors.

SERVICES

Remember, you are living an alternative lifestyle. As you get proficient at living this way, you will be able to help others make the jump. Along with your success stories, you will have the invaluable failures and mistakes that you can help others avoid.

Off grid consultation, mentoring and rescue are all great avenues for you to explore when providing services to real people.

. . .

You could help new off grid hopefuls find their piece of land, you could help off grid homesteaders improve their land or you could even rescue people who are flailing in the off grid lifestyle and are ready to call it quits. They might need counsel just like yours to help them get back on the horse.

The sky's the limit with this. You can even become hyper focused and just provide consultations on off grid power systems or raising goats successfully. It's all up to you.

OFF GRID INTERNET

High speed internet has opened a world of money making that is just too vast to ignore. We have to be honest with ourselves when we talk about the power of the internet and connect what we do to the millions of potential customers who might be looking for it.

Things are changing when it comes to the internet and it's important that we talk about that in this chapter. For a long time, people on rural off grid homesteads just assumed that high speed internet was not a possibility. However, there are people making money publishing YouTube videos from the middle of nowhere and it's very inspiring.

So, how do you go about getting yourself some high speed internet on your 40 acre off grid property?

. . .

First, begin the process of contacting all of your major providers. While you might assume they don't have high speed access in an area, you just won't know until you contact them.

We searched many properties when we were looking to upgrade our off grid situation. We had been lucky enough to have internet access on our first property. There were a number of very rural properties that surprised us. When you visit Verizon and Comcast's websites, you will be able to use the address to search for nearby service. We were pleasantly surprised on more than one occasion.

Let's look at some other options if you find out that you do not have access to high speed internet in the area of your off grid property.

Hughes Net

HughesNet is a satellite internet provider that covers all 50 states. It is a bit limited on speed and data caps, but that is going to be the case with any satellite internet. I have interviewed people on HughesNet who have sounded great and others who have been a garbled mess. Satellite internet is also affected by the weather.

- Download Speed: 25mbps
- Data Cap: 20G
- Installation Cost: $199

Rise Broadband

This fixed wireless service is available in 16 states and claims speeds up to 1000mbps! That is some high speed internet! If Rise is available in your area, I would highly recommend getting your hands on it. The data cap is massive, and this will make you feel like nothing has changed with internet service. In fact, some things might be even better!

- Download Speed: 5-1000mpbs
- Data Cap: 150GB
- Installation Cost: $149

Starlink

We have to discuss Elon Musk's bold initiative called Starlink. Personally, I know a handful of people who have signed up but none who are onboard yet. The claims are pretty strong, and I have to imagine that in time, Starlink will become an incredible opportunity for the off grid.

- Download Speed: 50-150mbps
- Data Cap: N/A
- Installation Cost: N/A

Century Link

Century Link is an impressive fixed wireless service that offers up 100mbps download speeds and a massive 1TB or terabyte per month data cap. The service is available in 36 states. Could be just the service you are looking for.

- Download Speed: 3-100mpb
- Data Cap: 1TB
- Installation Cost: $99

THE CULMINATION

The absolute best way to make money on an off grid homestead is to combine as many income streams as possible! It's not 1890 anymore so you don't have to depend solely on those fields and woods to make money. That said, you also do not need to be an off grid internet start to make it work. You can exist somewhere in the fray doing a bunch of things that you like and making money off all of them!

Perhaps you decide to break your annual income up over 5 different efforts! You could work remotely part time while growing food and animals, you can offer up consultation services in the evenings to people who want to get off grid and in your spare time, you can blacksmith little gifts to sell on Etsy.

While one of these ventures may not prove to be a sustaining income, altogether you will find yourself doing most of what you love and enjoying this new off grid life while making some money along the way!

CONCLUSION

You will never sleep like you sleep on your off grid homestead. The days wear you thin. Watching the molten sun dip into the horizon with a glass of sweet tea is a near meditative experience. The natural world is speaking all around you as crickets and cicadas come to life. Or maybe it's another season and it's hot coffee rather than cold tea. The earth falls to utter silence under a light accumulating snow.

I find myself listing all the things I am thankful for each night before I drift off. This has become something of a prayer for me. It's the promise of the next day that I love most of all. Watching the sun rise and the sun set, it's a reminder that you have sucked everything out of that day. You have lived your life to its fullest and now it's time to rest the mind and body.

When you are away from everything and existing in your own little off grid world, there is nothing like it. Of course, there will be parts about your old life that you miss, but mostly you will be building a new life that is full of satisfaction.

Do you think that the apex of humanity is to live a bubble wrapped life where everything we want, and need is delivered to our front door? I don't think that is where we were supposed to end up. It's just a frequency that is out of tune at the moment. We turned the knob on convenience a little too far to the right and now it's time to dial it back a bit.

Are you ready to be a part of that revolution?

The off grid lifestyle is well within your reach. If you have been playing with the idea of getting off grid, there is no time like the present. With this book as your guide, you should start having some conversations and doing some thinking about what it would really look like to pull the trigger on this new lifestyle.

In fact, I have a challenge for you. Visit a property. Seek out at least one off grid property or piece of land and go take a walk with a realtor. Take the ride, see the countryside and start fantasizing about what life might be like if you lived in your own off grid tiny home or cabin. There is something special about taking that ride and visiting a property.

Bring the book along with you, and as you walk the property start considering the things we discussed:

- Advantages & Disadvantages
- Location
- Permissions and Building
- Growing Food

- Powering the Location
- Making Money

Take the challenge. Your whole perspective will change when you take that drive and arrive at a fork in the road of your life. It will be scary, it will be exciting, but it could be the beginning of something incredible.

I hope I have conveyed the fact that this journey is no easy thing. It takes trimming away at what you think you need and maybe what you think you are. It takes hard work and planning. Things can fall through, so you must be prepared to face disappointment. However, even if you wind up falling flat in your efforts, you will at least be able to say you tried!

You never know, you might just arrive at true bliss.

FREE BONUS BOOK

**GET FREE, UNLIMITED ACCESS TO THIS BOOK
PLUS ALL OF OUR NEW BOOKS BY JOINING
THE ECO KOALA FAMILY**

JUST SCAN THE QR CODE BELOW

Made in the USA
Coppell, TX
13 August 2021

60439523R00108